KIY

[KNIT-IT-YOURSELF]

15 MODERN SWEATER DESIGNS TO STITCH AND WEAR

Emma Wright

Photography by Kim Lightbody

Hardie Grant

QUADRILLE

Square
022–063

Set-in
064–111

Raglan
112–153

INTRODUCTION

My journey with knitwear began like many of us, when I was taught to knit as a child by my Nan. I was always a very creative child. As a teenager, I knew I wanted to work in fashion, I knew I wanted to do something creative and work with my hands, so when I was 16 I went to college to study fashion and textiles. During my first year we made a hand knit project and all the knitting skills that I had learned as a child came flooding back to me, almost as if I had never stopped. I don't actually remember much about learning to knit; for me it's almost like I was born with these skills. After completing the project at college, I loved it so much that I taught myself how to crochet from books and videos online. I spent the whole of the summer between my first and second year knitting anything and everything I could. I had fallen in love and knew instantly that this was what I wanted to do.

For me, the beauty of knitting is in getting to create the fabric yourself, being able choose the fibre, colour, texture, and the pattern and individually creating each and every stitch with your own hands. I feel it's important to bring your own personality into everything you knit – even if you are following a pattern, choosing your own yarn and colour, or being able to change the length or the cast-on method is so important. This really allows you to knit something unique and is where the idea of this book began. I obsess over sweaters and I live in them throughout the winter, always pairing them with my favourite jeans. If I could, I would wear them all year round – and occasionally I do! I love the way that a sweater can easily be dressed up or down. I particularly love that knitting your own sweater fits in with the idea of slow fashion, which is so important in today's climate; that the sustainability of how the yarn is made, the fibre you choose and how it is dyed can be thoroughly thought out when choosing the yarn for your project. Every project that you knit is a blank canvas and a great opportunity to advance and further your skills.

HOW TO USE THIS BOOK

Welcome to my workshop! This book is a guide to help you master the three core sweater shapes, and then show you how to take your knitting further by developing your own designs. It is not a book for beginners – I am assuming you already know how to knit and already have a couple of projects under your belt.

Each project contains hints and tips to help achieve that perfect finish, but there is no better way to learn than the art of doing – practise makes perfect! Each pattern is a guide, so please feel free to apply your own cast on, cast (bind) off and sewing up techniques – unless it's otherwise stated in the pattern.

All the bodies and sleeves within the Square and Set-in sections are mix and match. For example, you can add the striped sleeves from Aster (pages 58–63) to the body of Pansy (pages 40–45), and pick your own pattern for the pockets. You can really get creative and knit it yourself! There are plenty of opportunities within the projects to design your own stripes, choose your own fabric patterns, and even mix and match yarn weights and colours. If you want to, add a DK (light worsted) weight sleeve to a chunky (bulky) weight body; or you can knit your sleeve plain, striped or with a cable – the possibilities are endless!

WHERE TO GET INSPIRATION

Sweaters are an investment. They are versatile and can be worn year-round so it's important to think about your starting point to get the end product that you want. For me, each design begins differently. I often take inspiration from the yarn itself: that may be the fibre, the colour, a particular collection of colour or texture. I like to wrap my knitting needles with the yarn when putting together a colour palette, which allows me to play with how the colours will go together and see what proportion of each colour will work best. I have included some blank models on page 154 for you to experiment with by creating your own sweater designs.

I always create a mood board when I'm making as it allows me to really get creative. Simply, scan can images you like from magazines, books or catalogues or print out images you've found online. Then pin these to a notice board or glue them down to a large piece of paper. Pinterest is also a really useful tool to create digital mood boards, using their collections of wonderfully inspiring imagery.

Once you have your mood board, on paper or digitally in the form of a Pinterest board, take time to really look through the images you have chosen. Is there a theme? Have you subconsciously picked out a colour palette or a yarn texture? These images will be the very starting point of your yarn project. Another great way to approach a project is to look at what's out on the high street or even what you already have in your wardrobe. Maybe you want your project to fit in with other items in your wardrobe or go with a specific outfit – or do you want to get creative? Learn a new technique? Or create something colourful that you can wear with jeans all year round? Once you've answered all these questions, have your mood board and a vague idea in your head, it's time to research your yarn. So visit physical stores, have a squeeze of the yarns that take your fancy, and get swatching.

YARNS

As mentioned in the inspiration section, knitting a sweater is an investment; each stitch takes time so first you want to spend time choosing the right yarn for your project. The ball band will give you a great deal of information, including: country of origin (which is helpful if you want to be environmentally friendly); weight of each ball; approx. length of yarn in the ball; what fibre the yarn is; and the shade and dye lot numbers. The length of yarn in each ball is important when substituting yarns – if your chosen yarn has a shorter length per ball than the yarn used in the pattern, you will need more balls to make the item. It's also important to buy balls in the same dye lot for your sweater – even with commercial manufacturers the colour can vary slightly over different dye lots.

Is there a specific fibre you want to work with? If you are looking for a neat smooth finish maybe try a merino or merino blend. Cotton and linen create great stitch definition, but don't have much stretch. Cashmere has a beautiful drape, or maybe try a wool or wool blend that has texture or a tweed effect. Yarn is not cheap so take your time to make long-lasting choices. Research the fibre you are working with to see if it suits the texture or pattern you have in mind. For example, if your project is fairisle you need a yarn with the right stitch definition and which has a solid colour. If the yarn is too textured or has colour shading or flecks, your pattern won't be as defined.

If your yarn comes in a hank (skein) you will need to wind it into a ball before you can use it to knit with. Untwist it and hang it on a chair back, then find a loose end and begin winding. Don't wind too tight or you will stretch the yarn.

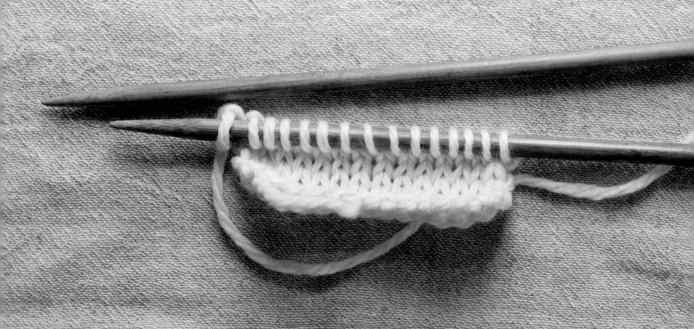

EQUIPMENT

NEEDLES

Everyone loves a beautiful bamboo needle; it looks the part on the WIP shot you'll post on Instagram. It also feels beautiful when you knit, passing each stitch from right to left needle. Many knitters don't realise that the material of the needle you knit with can massively affect your tension (gauge). Bamboo and wood needles tend to create a looser fabric, compared to plastic or metal needles. Always do a tension (gauge) swatch before beginning a project and adjust your needle size accordingly – if your swatch turns out bigger than stated in the pattern, you'll need to use smaller needles; if it turns out smaller, try going up a needle size. It's more important to match the stitch tension (or get it as close as you can) than the row tension.

Personally, I love to work with circular needles (bamboo or metal); they are lighter on your hands and wrists – perfect if this is something you struggle with. They are particularly great if you are someone who knits for long periods of time or for knitting on the train; no more elbowing the passenger sat next to you!

OTHER TOOLS

Other great things to have in your knit bag are, of course, scissors (a small sharp pair for snipping yarn), a ruler (if you can get a clear one with a grid, this is great for measuring tension (gauge) swatches), a tape measure, and stitch markers (or use short lengths of yarn and make little slip knots to place on your needles where needed). Other handy tools include a small crochet hook to help fix any mistakes, a large-eyed sewing needle and a notebook and pen to jot down any notes or amendments you make to the pattern as you go along.

Knitting Needle Sizes

Millimetre Range	U.S. Size Range
1.50 mm	000
1.75 mm	00
2 mm	0
2.25 mm	1
2.75 mm	2
3 mm	
3.125 mm	3
3.25 mm	3
3.50 mm	4
3.75 mm	5
4 mm	6
4.25 mm	6
4.50 mm	7
5 mm	8
5.25 mm	9
5.50 mm	9
5.75 mm	10
6 mm	10
6.50 mm	10 ½
7 mm	
8 mm	11
9 mm	13
10 mm	15
12.50 mm	17
12.75 mm	17
15 mm	19
19 mm	35
25 mm	50
35 mm	70

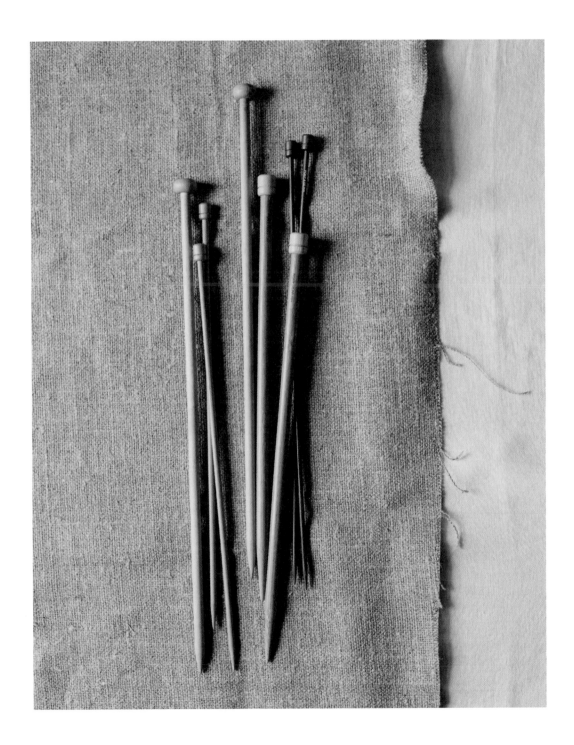

GARMENT CARE

If you have spent a lot of time and money creating your knitted sweater, you will want to be sure it is cared for properly so that it will last. The ball band on the yarn often has care instructions, so make sure that you note this information for the future – you could maybe take a photo of it with your phone or tablet. It's not necessary to wash a sweater every time you wear it – if it's not dirty but just has a slight odour, allow it to air for a few hours either hung up or laid flat on a towel, before putting it way.

It's usually best to hand-wash your hand-knitted sweaters. Keep dark and light colours separate, just in case colours do run when wet. Use warm water and mix it with a gentle detergent. Submerge the sweater and soak it for 10–15 minutes. Carefully rinse in warm water, then press out or squeeze to remove as much water as possible. Place the sweater flat on a dry towel, pulling it gently back into shape if necessary. Keep it away from sunlight and let it air dry at room temperature. Make sure the sweater is completely dry before putting it away.

Modern yarns – even wool – often have special finishes to make them machine-washable. If you are not sure, try machine-washing your tension (gauge) swatch first to see how it survives.

Store your sweaters folded neatly on a shelf or in a large drawer – it's not a good idea to hang them up for long periods, as the fabric will stretch over time.

ABBREVIATIONS

alt	alternative
approx.	approximately
beg	beginning
cont	continue
dec	decreas(e)ing
folls	follow(s)ing
inc	increas(e)ing
k	knit
k2tog	knit 2 stitches together
M1	make one stitch
M1p	make one stitch purlwise
p	purl
patt	pattern
p2tog	purl 2 stitches together
PM	place marker
prev	previous
psso	pass slipped st over
rem	remaining
rep	repeat(ed)
rev st st	reverse stocking (stockinette) stitch
RS	right side
sk2po	slip 1 stitch, knit 2 stitches together, pass slipped stitch over
sl	slip
SM	slip marker
ssk	slip, slip, knit
st(s)	stitch(es)
st st	stocking (stockinette) stitch
tog	together
WS	wrong side
yb	yarn back
yf	yarn forward
yo	yarn over needle
[ ]	work sequence in square brackets the number of times stated
*****	denotes beginning of repeated sequence of stitches

Square

A boxy garment uses the least amount of shaping – other than the neck decreases and sleeve increases it is knitted straight, creating a square silhouette. If you're a beginner at sweater knitting this is the best section to start with; I recommend Pansy (see pages 40–45) for your first sweater knit – it's a simple stitch and simple silhouette too!

Peony (see pages 52–57) is my favourite design from this section; I love brioche stitch, as although it's sometimes slow to grow it's definitely worth the effort. Another thing that makes this design great is being able to use some of my ever-growing button collection!

In this section you will work with stripes, learn the neatest way to shape a V-neck, create a shoulder button placket, knit honeycomb cable and add pockets. The body and sleeves of each pattern are easily mixed and matched – I am particularly found of mixing yarn weights. The chunky cabled body of Peony on page 54 or Violet on page 48 would look amazing with the simple sleeves from Magnolia (page 36) or the striped sleeve from Aster (page 62).

MAGNOLIA
[SQUARE | V-Neck]

PANSY

[SQUARE | Pocket Sweater]

PAGES 46–51

VIOLET

[SQUARE | Chunky Cable Sweater]

PEONY

[SQUARE | Brioche Buttoned Shoulder Sweater]

ASTER

[SQUARE | Striped Sweater]

MAGNOLIA
[SQUARE | V-Neck]

I find a neatly finished V-neck so satisfying. The direction of the decreases and the perfectly picked up stitches sit beautifully on the stocking (stockinette) stitch body of this sweater. If you wanted to make the design even simpler you could work the sleeves in stocking (stockinette) stitch only, too.

TECHNIQUE
V-neck shaping

SIZE Note sizes are approximate.

	Small	Medium	Large	X Large	XX Large	
To fit bust	81–86	91–96	101–106	112–117	122–127	cm
	32–34	36–38	40–42	44–46	48–50	in
Actual	120	130	140	150	160	cm
(approx.)	47¼	51¼	55	59	63	in
Length	54	54	58	60	64	cm
(approx.)	21¼	21¼	23	23½	25¼	in
Sleeve seam	43	45	47	47	49	cm
(approx.)	17	17¾	18½	18½	19¼	in

YARN
DK (light worsted)
Sample made in
The Fibre Co. Acadia
(60% Merino Wool, 20% Baby Alpaca, 20% Silk, approx. 133m/145yd per 50g/1¾oz hank)
9(**10**:11:**12**:12) hanks of Sand

NEEDLES AND OTHER ITEMS
4mm (US size 6) straight needles
4mm (US size 6) circular knitting needle (used straight)
2 stitch holders
Cable needle

TENSION (GAUGE)
22 sts x 30 rows = 10cm (4in) square working st st on 4mm (US size 6) needles.
13 sts = 4.5cm (1¾in) x 16 rows = 4cm (1½in) working cable on 4mm (US size 6) needles.

ABBREVIATIONS
See page 20

SPECIAL ABBREVIATIONS
C6B (cable 6 back): slip next 3 sts onto a cable needle and hold at back of work, k next 3 sts from left-hand needle and then k 3 sts from cable needle
C6F (cable 6 front): slip next 3 sts onto a cable needle and hold at front of work, k next 3 sts from left-hand needle and then k 3 sts from cable needle

MAKE

BACK

Using 4mm (US size 6) straight needles, cast on 134(**142**:154:**166**:178) sts.

Row 1 (RS): K2, *p2, k2; rep from * to end.

Row 2: P2, *k2, p2; rep from * to end.

These 2 rows rep form rib.

Cont in rib until work measures approx. 3cm (1¼in), ending with RS facing.

Now work st st as folls:

Row 1 (RS): K.

Row 2: P.

These 2 rows rep form st st. **

Cont in st st as set above until work measures approx. 54:**54**:58:**60**:64cm (21¼:**21¼**:23:**23½**:25¼in), ending with RS facing.

Shoulder shaping

Cast (bind) off 17(**17**:19:**21**:23) sts at beg of next 2 rows. *100(**108**:116:**124**:132) sts*

Cast (bind) off 15(**17**:19:**21**:23) sts at beg of next 4 rows. *40 sts*

Leave rem 40 sts on a holder at back neck.

FRONT

Work as for Back to **.

Cont in st st as set above until work measures approx. 30:**30**:33:**35**:37cm (11¾:**11¾**:13:**13¾**:14½in), ending with RS facing.

Split for V-neck

With RS facing, k across next 63(**67**:73:**79**:85) sts, turn work, place all rem sts on a holder.

Next row (WS): P.

V-neck shaping

With RS facing, begin V-neck shaping for left side of neck as folls:

Next row (dec, RS): K to last 4 sts, k2tog, k2. *62(**66**:72:**78**:84) sts*

Work 3 rows of st st.

These 4 rows including dec form V-neck dec, cont as set 15 times more until 47(**51**:57:**63**:69) sts rem, ending with RS facing.

Now work straight in st st only until work measures approx. 54:**54**:58:**60**:64cm (21¼:**21¼**:23:**23½**:25¼in), ending with RS facing.

Cast (bind) off 17(**17**:19:**21**:23) sts at beg of next row. *30(**34**:38:**42**:46) sts*

Cast (bind) off 15(**17**:19:**21**:23) sts at beg of next 2 rows.

Re-join yarn to sts left on a holder at front.

Cast (bind) off beg 8 sts at centre front neck (*63*:**67**:*73*:**79**:*85 sts* with first st on RH needle, keep that st on RH needle), k1, ssk, k to end. *62(**66**:72:**78**:84) sts*

Work 3 rows of st st.

Next row (dec, RS): K2, ssk, k to end. *61(**65**:71:**77**:83) sts*

Work 3 rows of st st.

These last 4 rows including dec form V-neck dec, cont as set 14 times more until 47(**51**:57:**63**:69) sts rem, ending with RS facing.

Now work straight in st st only until work measures approx. 54:**54**:58:**60**:64cm (21¼:**21¼**:23:**23½**:25¼in), ending with **WS** facing.

Cast (bind) off 17(**17**:19:**21**:23) sts at beg of next row. *30(**34**:38:**42**:46) sts*

Cast (bind) off 15(**17**:19:**21**:23) sts at beg of next 2 rows.

SLEEVES (make 2)

Using 4mm (US size 6) straight needles, cast on 42(**42**:46:**46**:50) sts.

Row 1 (RS): K2, *p2, k2; rep from * to end.

Row 2: P2, *k2, p2; rep from * to end.

These 2 rows rep form rib.

Cont in rib until work measures approx. 3cm (1¼in), ending with **WS** facing.

Next row (WS): P20(**20**:22:**22**:24), [M1p, p1] twice, M1p, p20(**20**:22:**22**:24). *45(**45**:49:**49**:53) sts*

Now work rev st st with centre cable as folls:

Row 1 (RS): P16(**16**:18:**18**:20), k13, p16(**16**:18:**18**:20).

Row 2: K16(**16**:18:**18**:20), p13, k16(**16**:18:**18**:20).

Rep last 2 rows once more.

Row 5: P16(**16**:18:**18**:20), C6F, k1, C6B, p16(**16**:18:**18**:20).

Row 6: As Row 2.

Row 7: P1, M1p, p15(**15**:17:**17**:19), k13, p15(**15**:17:**17**:19), M1p, p1. *47(47:51:51:55) sts*

Row 8: K17(**17**:19:**19**:21), p13, k17(**17**:19:**19**:21).

Row 9: P17(**17**:19:**19**:21), k13, p17(**17**:19:**19**:21).

Rep last 2 rows once more.

Row 12: K17(**17**:19:**19**:21), p13, k17(**17**:19:**19**:21).

Row 13: P1, M1p, p16(**16**:18:**18**:20), C6B, k1, C4F, p16(**16**:18:**18**:20), M1p, p1. *49(**49**:53:**53**:57) sts*

Row 14: K18(**18**:20:**20**:22), p13, k18(**18**:20:**20**:22).

Row 15: P18(**18**:20:**20**:22), k13, p18(**18**:20:**20**:22).

Row 16: K18(**18**:20:**20**:22), p13, k18(**18**:20:**20**:22).

These 16 rows rep form rev st st with centre cable and inc every 6th row.

Cont as set above WHILST AT THE SAME TIME working inc at each end of every 6th row to 81(**81**:89:**89**:97) sts, ending with RS facing.

Cont straight in rev st st with centre cable only, until work measures approx. 43:**45**:47:**47**:49cm (17:**17¾**:18½:**18½**:19¼in), ending with RS facing.

Cast (bind) off.

FINISHING

Press/block all garment pieces.
Join shoulder seams.

Neckband

Using 4mm (US size 6) circular needle and beginning at bottom of right front shaping (not across 8 st cast (bind) off at front neck) pick up and k 73(**73**:77:**77**:81) sts up right front neck to right shoulder seam, re-join yarn and k 40 sts across back neck and then pick up and k 73(**73**:77:**77**:81) sts down left front neck ending before 8 st cast (bind) off at front neck. *186(**186**:194:**194**:202) sts*

Next row (WS): P2, *k2, p2; rep from * to end.

Next row: K2, *p2, k2; rep from * to end.

These last 2 rows form rib.

Cont in rib until neckband measures approx. 3.5cm (1½in), ending with RS facing.

Cast (bind) off in rib.

Join beg/end of neckband across 8-st cast (bind) off at front neck by overlapping end of right front neckband over the left (use photograph as guide if needed).

Join centre of sleeve cast (bind) off to shoulder seam and sew sleeve approx. 18:**18**:20:**20**:22cm (7:**7**:8:**8**:8¾in) down each side of shoulder seam; rep for second sleeve. Join side and sleeve seam. Press/block again if needed.

HINTS AND TIPS

▶ Working k2tog on the right side of the neck shaping and ssk on the left side of the neck shaping allows the stitches to sit in the right direction for a neater finish.

◉ Working the shaping decreases a few stitches into the work instead of over the last two stitches at the edge will create a neater decrease and will also allow a neater pick up for the neckband.

◗ Use your right-hand needle only when picking up stitches; insert that needle into the work where you want your stitch picked up, wrap the yarn around the needle and bring the stitch through the work (stitch picked up!). Picking up stitches this way will stop holes, so there is no need to knit into the back of the stitch.

◆ When picking up stitches along an edge, insert the needle (see picking up method above) one stitch into the work rather than into the stitch that's right at the edge.

PANSY

[SQUARE | Pocket Sweater]

If you're a pattern lover but don't really like wearing pattern all over this is the sweater for you. Choose between checked (shown in the photographs), hounds tooth or leopard print pockets, mix and match yarn weights or pick your own colour palette. This is a real knit-it-yourself sweater!

TECHNIQUE
Adding pockets to a garment – three options

SIZE Note sizes are approximate.

	Small	Medium	Large	X Large	XX Large	
To fit	81–86	91–96	101–106	112–117	122–127	cm
	32–34	36–38	40–42	44–46	48–50	in
Actual	122	130	140	148	162	cm
(approx.)	48	51¼	55	58¼	63¾	in
Length	54	54	56	58	62	cm
(approx.)	21¼	21¼	22	23	24½	in
Sleeve seam	43	45	47	47	49	cm
(approx.)	17	17¾	18½	18½	19¼	in

YARN
Aran (worsted)
Sample made in
MillaMia Naturally Soft Aran
(100% Extrafine Merino Wool, approx.
80m/87yd per 50g/1¾oz ball)
16(**17**:18:**20**:22) balls of Ice (**A**)
1(**1**:1:**1**:1) balls of Blush (**B**)
Pocket option one – checked
1 ball of contrast yarn (**C**)
Pocket option two – houndstooth
1 ball each of 2 contrast yarns (**D** & **E**)
Pocket option three – leopard print
1 ball each of 3 contrast chunky (bulky)
yarns (**F**, **G** & **H**)

NEEDLES AND OTHER ITEMS
5mm (US size 8) knitting needles
2 stitch holders
Yarn needle
10mm (US size 15) knitting needles
(pocket option three only)

TENSION (GAUGE)
18 sts x 24 rows = 10cm (4in) square
working st st on 5mm (US size 8) needles.
18 sts x 36 rows = 10cm (4in) square
working garter st on 5mm (US size 8)
needles.

ABBREVIATIONS
See page 20

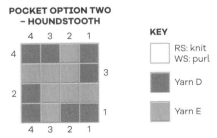

**POCKET OPTION TWO
– HOUNDSTOOTH**

KEY

☐ RS: knit
WS: purl

◼ Yarn D

◼ Yarn E

MAKE

BACK
Using 5mm (US size 8) needles and A,
cast on 110(**118**:126:**134**:146) sts.
Row 1 (RS): K2, *p2, k2; rep from * to end.
Row 2: P2, *k2, p2; rep from * to end.
These 2 rows rep form rib.
Cont in rib until work measures approx.
3.5cm (1½in), ending with RS facing.
Now work garter st as folls:
Row 1 (RS): K.
Row 2: K.
These 2 rows rep form garter st. **
Cont in garter st as set above until work
measures approx. 54:**54**:56:**56**:60cm
(21¼:**21¼**:22:**22**:23½in), ending with RS facing.
Shoulder shaping
Cast (bind) off 13(**14**:15:**17**:19) sts at beg of next
4 rows. *58(**62**:66:**66**:70) sts*
Cast (bind) off 13(**15**:17:**17**:19) sts at beg of next
2 rows. *32 sts*
Leave rem 32 sts on a holder at back neck.

FRONT
Work as for Back to **.
Cont in garter st as set above until work measures
approx. 48(**48**:50:**50**:54cm (19:**19**:19¾:**19¾**:21¼in),
ending with RS facing.
Front neck shaping
With RS facing and keeping garter st correct
work over next 49(**53**:57:**61**:67) sts, turn work,
leaving all rem sts on a st holder.
Left front neck
Next row (WS): Cast (bind) off 6 sts, k to end.
*43(**47**:51:**55**:61) sts*
Work RS row.
Next row (WS): Cast (bind) off 3 sts, k to end.

*40(**44**:48:**52**:58) sts*
Work RS row.
Next row (WS): K2tog, k to end. *39(**43**:47:**51**:57) sts*
Now cont straight in garter st until work measures
approx. 54:**54**:56:**56**:60cm (21¼:**21¼**:22:**22**:23½in),
ending with RS facing.
Left shoulder shaping
Next row (RS): Cast (bind) off 13(**14**:15:**17**:19) sts,
k to end. *26(**29**:32:**34**:38) sts*
Work **WS** row.
Next row (RS): Cast (bind) off 13(**14**:15:**17**:19) sts,
k to end. *13(**15**:17:**17**:19) sts*
Work **WS** row.
Cast (bind) off rem 13(**15**:17:**17**:19) sts.
Centre and right front neck
With RS facing of sts left on a holder, keep
centre 12 sts at front neck on a holder and
work on rem 49(**53**:57:**61**:67) sts as folls:
Next row (RS): Cast (bind) off 6 sts, k to end.
*43(**47**:51:**55**:61) sts*
Work **WS** row.
Next row (RS): Cast (bind) off 3 sts, k to end.
*40(**44**:48:**52**:58) sts*
Work **WS** row.
Next row (RS): K2tog, k to end. *39(**43**:47:**51**:57) sts*
Now cont straight in garter st until work measures
approx. 54:**54**:56:**56**:60cm (21¼:**21¼**:22:**22**:23½in),
ending with RS facing.
Right shoulder shaping
Next row (RS): Cast (bind) off 13(**15**:15:**17**:18) sts,
k to end. *26(**29**:32:**34**:38) sts*
Work **WS** row.
Next row (RS): Cast (bind) off 13(**15**:15:**17**:18) sts,
k to end. *13(**15**:17:**17**:19) sts*
Work **WS** row.
Cast (bind) off rem 13(**15**:17:**17**:19) sts.

SLEEVES (make 2)

Using 5mm (US size 8) needles and A, cast on 38(**38**:42:**42**:46) sts.
Row 1 (RS): K.
Row 2: K.
Work these 2 rows once more.
Now work st st as folls:
Row 1 (RS): K.
Row 2: P.
These 2 rows rep form st st.
Cont in st st as set above WHILST AT THE SAME TIME inc 1 st at each end of next and then every eighth row to 58(**58**:62:**62**:66) sts, ending with RS facing.
Cont straight in st st until work measures approx. 43:**45**:47:**47**:49cm (17:**17¾**:18½:**18½**:19¼in), ending with RS facing.
Cast (bind) off.

POCKETS (make 2)

Option one – Checked

Using 5mm (US size 8) needles and B, cast on 30 sts using the long tail cast-on method.
Next row: P5 B, *[p1 C, p1 B] twice; rep from * to last 5 sts, p5 B.
Next row (RS): K5 B, *[k1 C, k1 B] twice; rep from * to last 5 sts, k5 B.
Next row: P5 B, *[p1 C, p1 B] twice; rep from * to last 5 sts, p5 B.
Now work in checked patt as folls:
**Next row: [K1 B, k1 C] twice, k1 B, *k4 C, [k1 C, k1 B] twice; rep from * to last st, k1 B.
Next row: P1 B, *[p1 C, p1 B] twice, p4 C; rep from * to last 5 sts, [p1 C, p1 B] twice, p1 B.
Rep last 2 rows once more.
Next row: K5 B, *[k1 C, k1 B] twice; rep from * to last 5 sts, k5 B.
Next row: P5 B, *[p1 C, p1 B] twice; rep from * to last 5 sts, p5 B.

Rep last 2 rows once more.
These 8 rows from ** form patt.
Rep from ** until pocket measures approx. 11cm (4¼in), ending with RS facing.
Cont in B only.
Work 4 rows of k.
Cast (bind) off.

Option two – Houndstooth

Using 5mm (US size 8) needles and D, cast on 32 sts with the long tail cast-on method.
Next row: P.
Now work houndstooth fairisle (using chart from page 137 if needed) as folls:
Row 1 (RS): *K2 D, k1 E, k1 D; rep from * to end.
Row 2: *P1 D, p3 E; rep from * to end.
Row 3: *K1 D, k3 E; rep from * to end.
Row 4: *P2 D, p1 E, p1 D; rep from * to end.
These 4 rows rep form houndstooth fairisle.
Cont in houndstooth until pocket measures approx. 11cm (4¼in), ending with RS facing.
Cont in E only.
Work 4 rows of k.
Cast (bind) off.

Option three – leopard print

Using 10mm (US size 15) needles and chunky (bulky) yarn F, cast-on 18 sts with the long tail cast on method.
Next row: P.
Now follow Leopard Chart opposite completing all 17 rows in F and G.
Cont in F only.
Next row: P.
Work 4 rows of k.
Cast (bind) off.
Using H threaded in a yarn needle, work Swiss darn/duplicate stitches as indicated on the Leopard Print Chart.

POCKET OPTION THREE – LEOPARD PRINT

KEY

☐ Knit	
▦ Yarn F	
■ Yarn G	
● Swiss darn/ duplicate stitch using yarn H	

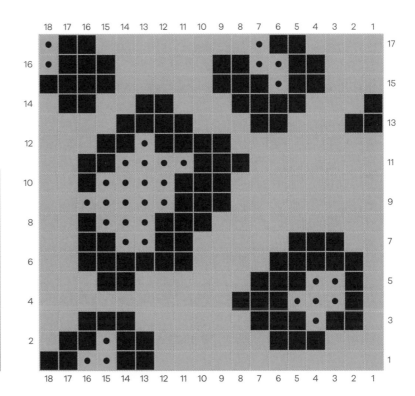

HINTS AND TIPS

▶ Use pins to get the pockets in the correct position before sewing them on.

◉ Use mattress stitch to sew the pockets into place to create a neat finish.

FINISHING

Press/block all garment pieces.
Join left shoulder seam.

Neckband

Using 5mm (US size 8) needles and B, re-join yarn to and k 32 sts left on a holder at back neck, pick up and k 13 sts down left front neck, re-join yarn to 12 sts left on a holder at front neck, and then pick up and k 13 sts up right front neck. *70 sts*

Next row (WS): P2, *k2, p2; rep from * to end.
Next row: K2, *p2, k2; rep from * to end.
These last 2 rows form rib.
Cont in rib until neckband measures approx. 3.5cm (1½in), ending with RS facing.
Cast (bind) off in rib.
Join right shoulder and neckband seam.
Join centre of sleeve cast (bind) off to shoulder seam and sew sleeve approx. 18:**18**:20:**20**:22cm (7:**7**:8:**8**:8¾in) down each side of shoulder seam, rep for second sleeve. Join side and sleeve seams. Sew a pair of pockets to garment front, using photograph as a guide for placement.
Press/block again if needed.

VIOLET

[SQUARE | Chunky Cable Sweater]

Honeycomb cable is a favourite texture of mine, almost a guilty pleasure. I think the constant cabling is worth the effort for that final look. In this garment the honeycomb is broken up into two sections for a more enjoyable knit. If you like the idea of mixing yarn weights you can take the sleeves from Magnolia (see page 36) and sew them onto the chunky body of this sweater.

TECHNIQUE
Honeycomb cable

SIZE Note sizes are approximate.

	Small	Medium	Large	
To fit	81–86	101–106	122–127	cm
	32–34	40–42	48–50	in
Actual	124	144	164	cm
(approx.)	48¾	56¾	64½	in
Length	52	54	58	cm
(approx.)	20½	21¼	23	in
Sleeve seam	43	45	47	cm
(approx.)	17	17¾	18½	in

YARN
Super chunky (super bulky)
Sample made in
Debbie Bliss Paloma Tweed
(50% Alpaca, 30% Wool, 14% Acrylic,
6% Viscose, approx. 65m/71yd per
50g/1¾oz ball)
14(**16**:17) balls of Amethyst

NEEDLES AND OTHER ITEMS
10mm (US size 15) knitting needles
Cable needle
2 stitch holders

TENSION (GAUGE)
12 sts x 18 rows = 10cm (4in) square working st st on 10mm (US size 15) needles.

16 sts x 20 rows = 10cm (4in) square working honeycomb cable on 10mm (US size 15) needles.

ABBREVIATIONS
See page 20

SPECIAL ABBREVIATIONS
C4B (cable 4 back): slip next 2 sts onto a cable needle and hold at back of work, k next 2 sts from left-hand needle and then k 2 sts from cable needle
C4F (cable 4 front): slip next 2 sts onto a cable needle and hold at front of work, k next 2 sts from left-hand needle and then k 2 sts from cable needle

MAKE

BACK
Using 10mm (US size 15) needles, cast on 98(**114**:130) sts.
Row 1 (RS): *K1, p1; rep from * to end.
Row 2: As Row 1.
Work these 2 rows three times more.
Now work in cable patt as folls:
Row 1 (RS): K32(**40**:48), p1, k4, p8, k8, p8, k4, p1, k32(**40**:48).
Row 2: P32(**40**:48), k1, p4, k8, p8, k8, p4, k1, p32(**40**:48).
Row 3: [C4B, C4F] 4(**5**:6) times, p1, C4B, p8, C4B, C4F, p8, C4B, p1, [C4B, C4F] 4(**5**:6) times.
Row 4: As Row 2.
Row 5: As Row 1.
Row 6: As Row 2.
Row 7: [C4F, C4B] 4(**5**:6) times, p1, C4B, p8, C4B, C4F, p8, C4B, p1, [C4F, C4B] 4(**5**:6) times.
Row 8: As Row 2.
These 8 rows rep form cable patt. **
Cont in cable patt until work measures approx. 52:**54**:58cm (20½:**21¼**:23in), ending with RS facing.
Shoulder shaping
Cast (bind) off 12(**15**:18) sts at beg of next 4 rows. 50(**54**:58) sts
Cast (bind) off 14(**16**:18) sts at beg of next 2 rows. 22(**22**:22) sts
Leave rem 22 sts on a holder at back neck.

FRONT
Work as for Back to **.
Cont in cable patt until work measures approx. 44(**46**:50cm (17¼:**18**:19¾in), ending with RS facing.
Front neck shaping
With RS facing and keeping cable patt correct throughout, work over next 45(**53**:61) sts, turn

work leaving all rem sts on a st holder.
Left front neck
Next row (WS): Cast (bind) off 3 sts, cable patt to end. *42(**50**:58) sts*
Work RS row in cable patt.
Next row (WS): Cast (bind) off 2 sts, cable patt to end. *40(**48**:56) sts*
Work RS row in cable patt.
Next row (WS): Cast (bind) off 2 sts, cable patt to end. *38(**46**:54) sts*
Now work straight in cable patt until work measures approx. 52:**54**:58cm (20½:**21¼**:23in) from cast-on edge, ending with RS facing.
Left shoulder shaping
Next 2 alt rows (RS): Cast (bind) off 12(**15**:18) sts, cable patt to end. *14(**16**:18) sts*
Work **WS** row in cable patt.
Cast (bind) off rem 14(**16**:18) sts.
Centre and right front neck
With RS facing, keep centre 8 sts at front neck on a holder and work on rem 45(**53**:61) sts as folls:
Next row (RS): Cast (bind) off 3 sts, cable to end. *42(**50**:58) sts*
Work **WS** row in cable patt.
Next row (RS): Cast (bind) off 2 sts, cable to end. *40(**48**:56) sts*
Work **WS** row in cable patt.
Next row (RS): Cast (bind) off 2 sts, cable to end. *38(**46**:54) sts*
Now work straight in cable patt until work measures approx. 52:**54**:58cm (20½:**21¼**:23in) from cast-on edge, ending with **WS** facing.
Right shoulder shaping
Next 2 alt rows (WS): Cast (bind) off 12(**15**:18) sts, cable patt to end. *14(**16**:18) sts*
Work **RS** row in cable patt.
Cast (bind) off rem 14(**16**:18) sts.

SLEEVES (make 2)

Using 10mm (US size 15) needles, cast on 24(**26**:30) sts.

Row 1 (RS): *K1, p1; rep from * to end.

Row 2: As Row 1.

Work these 2 rows three times more.

Now work in st st as folls:

Row 1 (RS): K.

Row 2: P.

These 2 rows rep form st st.

Cont in st st as set above WHILST AT THE SAME TIME in 1 st at each end of next and then every fourth row to 44(**46**:50) sts, ending with RS facing.

Cont straight in st st until work measures approx. 43:**45**:47cm (17:**17¾**:18½in), ending with RS facing.

Cast (bind) off.

FINISHING

Press/block all garment pieces.

Join left shoulder seam.

Neckband

Using 10mm (US size 15) needles, re-join yarn to 22 sts left on a holder at back neck, pick up and k 10 sts down left front neck, re-join yarn to 8 sts left on a holder at front neck, then pick up and k 10 sts up right front neck. *50(**50**:50) sts*

Next row (WS): *K1, p1; rep from * to end.

This row rep forms rib.

Cont in rib until neckband measures approx. 5cm (2in), ending with RS facing.

Cast (bind) off in rib.

Join right shoulder and neckband seam.

Join centre of sleeve cast (bind) off to shoulder seam and sew sleeve approx. 18:**20**:22cm (7:**8**:8¾in) down each side of shoulder seam; rep for second sleeve. Join side and sleeve seam.

Press/block again if needed.

HINTS AND TIPS

▶ Make sure you do a tension (gauge) swatch for the honeycomb cable and adjust your needle size if necessary to match the tension (gauge) in the pattern. We all hold our yarn and needles so differently and it's important to get the honeycomb cable correct so that your final fabric isn't too tight.

❍ Use a cable needle if necessary when working your honeycomb cable; if you don't have one you can use a pencil.

PEONY

[SQUARE | Brioche Buttoned Shoulder Sweater]

If, like me, your button box doesn't close over your never-ending button collection this is the perfect project to use some! Putting together a little collection of different shapes, colours and sizes of buttons is pretty satisfying, and you could also try sewing them on with different coloured scraps of yarn from your stash.

TECHNIQUE
Brioche stitch and adding buttons from your collection

SIZE Note sizes are approximate.

	Small	Medium	Large	X Large	XX Large	
To fit	81–86	91–96	101–106	112–117	122–127	cm
	32–34	36–38	40–42	44–46	48–50	in
Actual	120	130	140	150	160	cm
(approx.)	47¼	51¼	55	59	63	in
Length	52	54	54	56	58	cm
(approx.)	20½	21¼	21¼	22	23	in
Sleeve seam	43	45	47	47	49	cm
(approx.)	17	17¾	18½	18½	19¼	in

YARN
Super chunky (super bulky)
Sample made in
Erika Knight Maxi Wool
(100% Wool, approx. 80m/88yd
per 100g/3½oz hank)
8(**9**:9:**10**:11) hanks of Chaos

NEEDLES AND OTHER ITEMS
10mm (US size 15) knitting needles
4 stitch holders
6 assorted buttons from your collection

TENSION (GAUGE)
10 sts x 24 rows = 10cm (4in) square
working brioche st on 10mm (US size 15)
needles.

ABBREVIATIONS
See page 20

SPECIAL ABBREVIATIONS
BK2tog (brioche 2 sts together):
k tog next st with its paired over
from prev row
YOS (yarn over slipped stitch):
bring yarn over right-hand needle

MAKE

BACK

Using 10mm (US size 15) needles, cast on 61(**65**:71:**75**:81) sts.

Row 1 (RS): K1, *p1, k1; rep from * to end.

Row 2: P1, *k1, p1; rep from * to end.

Work these 2 rows once more.

Now work brioche st as folls:

Brioche set up row: K1, *yf, sl 1 purlwise, YOS, k1; rep from * to end.

Brioche row 1 (WS): *Yf, sl 1 purlwise, YOS, BK2tog; rep from * to last st, yf, sl 1 purlwise.

Brioche row 2 (RS): K1, *yf, sl 1 purlwise, YOS, BK2tog; rep from * to end.

These 2 rows rep form brioche st. **

Cont in brioche st as set above until work measures approx. 52:**54**:54:**56**:58cm (20½:**21¼**:21¼:**22**:23in), ending with **WS** facing.

Shoulder shaping

Note: See hints and tips before casting (binding) off.

Place next 21(**23**:26:**28**:31) sts on a holder, work to end.

Cast (bind) off 21(**23**:26:**28**:31) sts, work to end. *19 sts*

Leave rem 19 sts on a second holder at back neck.

FRONT

Work as for Back to **.

Cont in brioche st as set above until work measures approx. 44:**46**:46:**48**:50cm (17¼:**18**:18:**19**:19¾in), ending with RS facing.

Front neck shaping

With RS facing and keeping brioche st correct throughout, work over next 26(**28**:31:**33**:36) sts, turn work, leaving all rem sts on a st holder.

Left front neck

Next row (WS): Cast (bind) off 2 sts, brioche st to end. *24(**26**:29:**31**:34) sts*

Work RS row in brioche st.

Next row (WS): Cast (bind) off 2 sts, brioche st to end. *22(**24**:27:**29**:32) sts*

Work RS row in brioche st.

Next row (WS): K2tog, brioche st to end. *21(**23**:26:**28**:31) sts*

Now work straight in brioche st until work measures approx. 49:**51**:51:**53**:55cm (19¼:**20**:20:**21**:21½in), ending with RS facing.

Leave these sts on a third holder.

Centre and right front neck

With RS facing and keeping brioche st correct, keep centre 9 sts at front neck on a fourth holder and work on rem 26(**28**:31:**33**:36) sts as folls:

Next row (RS): Cast (bind) off 2 sts, brioche st to end. *24(**26**:29:**31**:34) sts*

Work **WS** row in brioche st.

Next row (RS): Cast (bind) off 2 sts, brioche st to end. *22(**24**:27:**29**:32) sts*

Work **WS** row in brioche st.

Next row (RS): K2tog, brioche st to end. *21(**23**:26:**28**:31) sts*

Now work straight in brioche st until work measures approx. 52:**54**:54:**56**:58cm (20½:**21¼**:21¼:**22**:23in), ending with RS facing.

Cast (bind) off in rib.

SLEEVES (make 2)

Using 10mm (US size 15) needles, cast on 21(**21**:23:**23**:25) sts.

Row 1 (RS): K1, *p1, k1; rep from * to end.

Row 2: P1, *k1, p1; rep from * to end.

Work these 2 rows once more.

Now work brioche st as folls:

Brioche set up row: K1, *yf, sl 1 purlwise, YOS, k1; rep from * to end.

Brioche row 1 (WS): *Yf, sl 1 purlwise, YOS, BK2tog; rep from * to last st, yf, sl 1 purlwise.

Brioche row 2 (RS): K1, *yf, sl 1 purlwise, YOS, BK2tog; rep from * to end.

These 2 rows rep form brioche st.

Cont in brioche st as set above WHILST AT THE SAME TIME inc 1 st at each end of next and then every 16th row to 33(**33**:35:**35**:37) sts, ending with RS facing.

Cont straight in brioche st until work measures approx. 43(**45**:47:**47**:49cm (17(**17¾**:18½:**18½**:19¼in), ending with RS facing.

Cast (bind) off.

FINISHING

Press/block all garment pieces.

Join right shoulder seam.

Neckband

Using 10mm (US size 15) needles and with **WS** of back facing, pick up and p 19 sts across back, pick up and p 9 sts down right front neck, re-join yarn to 9 sts left on a holder at front neck and then pick up and p 9 sts up left front neck. *46 sts*

Next row (RS): *K1, p1; rep from * to end.

Next row: *P1, k1; rep from * to end.

These last 2 rows form rib.

Cont in rib until neckband measures approx. 5cm (2in), ending with RS facing.

Cast (bind) off in rib.

Button placket

Using 10mm (US size 15) needles and with RS of back facing, beg at neckband, pick up and k 20 sts across neckband and shoulder.

Next row (WS): *P2, k2; rep from * to end.

This last row ONLY forms rib, rep it four more times, ending with RS facing.

Cast (bind) off.

Buttonhole placket

Using 10mm (US size 15) needles and with RS of front facing, pick up and k 20 sts across neckband and shoulder.

Next row (WS): *P2, k2; rep from * to end.

This last row ONLY forms rib.

Next row: Work 2 sts in rib, cast (bind) off 2 sts, *work 1 st in rib, cast (bind) off 2 sts; rep from * to last st, work last st in rib.

Work 2 more rows of rib, ending with RS facing.

Cast (bind) off.

Join centre of sleeve cast (bind) off to shoulder seam and sew sleeve approx. 18(**18**:20:**20**:22cm (7(**7**:8:**8**:8¾in) down each side of shoulder seam; rep for second sleeve. Join side and sleeve seam.

Sew 6 buttons to button placket in line with buttonholes on buttonhole placket.

Press/block again if needed.

HINTS AND TIPS

▸ When working brioche stitches remember to always treat each knit stitch and its paired yarn over (YO) as one stitch, especially when increasing, decreasing and casting (binding) off.

● Take your time when working the brioche stitch; it's not the easiest stitch to undo so take extra care when increasing, decreasing and casting (binding) off.

ASTER

[SQUARE | Striped Sweater]

Stripes look chic in every fabric but I think especially in knitwear – we all love a knitted stripe! The amazing thing about this project is that you can decide which stripe sequence you prefer – have fun swatching them all before you decide.

TECHNIQUE
Working with stripes

SIZE Note sizes are approximate.

	Small	Medium	Large	X Large	XX Large	
To fit	81–86	91–96	101–106	112–117	122–127	cm
	32–34	36–38	40–42	44–46	48–50	in
Actual	130	140	150	160	170	cm
(approx.)	51¼	55	59	63	67	in
Length	53	53	57	59	63	cm
(approx.)	21	21	22½	23¼	24¾	in
Sleeve seam	43	45	47	47	49	cm
(approx.)	17	17¾	18½	18½	19¼	in

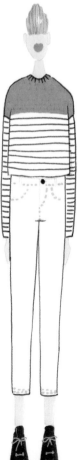

YARN
DK (light worsted)
Sample made in
Rico Essentials Merino DK
(100% Merino Wool, approx. 120m/131yd per 50g/1¾oz ball)
6(**7**:8:**9**:10) balls of Natural (**A**)
3(**3**:4:**5**:6) balls of Black (**B**)
3(**4**:5:**6**:6) balls of Brick Red (**C**)

NEEDLES AND OTHER ITEMS
4mm (US size 6) knitting needles
2 stitch holders

TENSION (GAUGE)
22 sts x 28 rows = 10cm (4in) square working st st on 4mm (US size 6) needles.
17 sts x 35 rows = 10cm (4in) square working moss (seed) st on 4mm (US size 6) needles.

ABBREVIATIONS
See page 20

MAKE

BACK

Using 4mm (US size 6) needles and A, cast on 143(**154**:165:**176**:187) sts.

Row 1 (RS): K.

Row 2: K.

Work these 2 rows once more.

Now work striped st st (or see stripe alternatives on page 62) as folls:

Row 1 (RS): K.

Row 2: P.

Work these 2 rows once more.

Change to B.

Row 5: K.

Row 6: P.

Change to A.

These 6 rows rep form striped st st.

Cont in striped st st as set above until work measures approx. 34:**34**:36:**38**:40cm (13½:**13½**:14:**15**:15¾in), ending with Row 4 of striped st st patt and RS facing.

Next row (RS): K7(**10**:10:**9**:9), [k2:**2**:**2**:**2**:2, k2tog] 32(**33**:36:**39**:42) times, k8(**12**:11:**11**:10). *111(**121**:129:**137**:145) sts*

Change to C.

Next row (WS): P.

Now work in moss (seed) st as folls:

Row 1 (RS): K1, *p1, k1; rep from * to end.

This row rep forms moss (seed) st. **

Cont in moss (seed) st as set above until work measures approx. 18:**18**:20:**20**:22cm (7:**7**:8:**8**:8¾in) from colour change to C, ending with RS facing.

Shoulder shaping

Cast (bind) off 13(**15**:15:**17**:18) sts at beg of next 4 rows. *59(**61**:69:**69**:73) sts*

Cast (bind) off 14(**15**:17:**17**:18) sts at beg of next 2 rows. *31(**31**:35:**35**:37) sts*

Leave rem 31(**31**:35:**35**:37) sts on a holder at back neck.

FRONT

Work as for Back to **.

Cont in moss (seed) st as set above until work measures approx. 13:**13**:15:**15**:17cm (5 ⅛:**5 ⅛**:6:**6**:6¾in) from colour change to C, ending with RS facing.

Front neck shaping

With RS facing and keeping moss (seed) st correct throughout, work over next 49(**54**:56:**60**:63) sts, turn work, leaving all rem sts on a st holder.

Left front neck

Next row (WS): Cast (bind) off 5 sts, moss (seed) st to end. *44(**49**:51:**55**:58) sts*

Work RS row in moss (seed) st.

Next row (WS): Cast (bind) off 3 sts, moss (seed) st to end. *41(**46**:48:**52**:55) sts*

Work RS row in moss (seed) st.

Next row (WS): P2tog, moss (seed) st to end. *40(**45**:47:**51**:54) sts*

Now work straight in moss (seed) st until work measures approx. 18:**18**:20:**20**:22cm (7:**7**:8:**8**:8¾in) from colour change to C, ending with RS facing.

Left shoulder shaping

Next row (RS): Cast (bind) off 13(**15**:15:**17**:18) sts, moss (seed) st to end. *27(**30**:32:**34**:36) sts*

Work **WS** row in moss (seed) st.

Next row (RS): Cast (bind) off 13(**15**:15:**17**:18) sts, moss (seed) st to end. *14(**15**:17:**17**:18) sts*

Work **WS** row in moss (seed) st.

Cast (bind) off rem 14(**15**:17:**17**:18) sts.

Centre and right front neck

With RS facing of sts left on a holder, keep centre 13(**13**:17:**17**:19) sts at front neck on a holder and work on rem 49(**54**:56:**60**:63) sts as folls:

Next row (RS): Cast (bind) off 5 sts, moss (seed) st to end. *44(**49**:51:**55**:58) sts*

Work **WS** row in moss (seed) st.

Next row (RS): Cast (bind) off 3 sts, moss (seed) st to end. *41(46:48:52:55) sts*

Work **WS** row in moss (seed) st.

Next row (RS): K2tog, moss (seed) st to end. *40(45:47:51:54) sts*

Now work straight in moss (seed) st until work measures approx. 18:**18**:20:**20**:22cm (7:**7**:8:**8**:8¾in) from colour change to C, ending with **WS** facing.

Right shoulder shaping

Next row (WS): Cast (bind) off 13(**15**:15:**17**:18) sts, moss (seed) st to end. *27(30:32:34:36) sts*

Work RS row in moss (seed) st.

Next row (WS): Cast (bind) off 13(**15**:15:**17**:18) sts, moss (seed) st to end. *14(15:17:17:18) sts*

Work RS row in moss (seed) st.

Cast (bind) off rem 14(**15**:17:**17**:18) sts.

SLEEVES (make 2)

Using 4mm (US size 6) needles and A, cast on 40(**40**:44:**44**:48) sts.

Row 1 (RS): K.

Row 2: K.

Rep these 2 rows once more.

Now work striped st st as folls:

Row 1 (RS): K.

Row 2: P.

Work these 2 rows once more.

Change to B.

Row 5: K.

Row 6: P.

Change to A.

These 6 rows rep form striped st st.

Cont in striped st st as set above WHILST AT THE SAME TIME inc 1 st at each end of next and then every fourth row to 80(**80**:88:**88**:96) sts, ending with RS facing.

Cont straight in st st until work measures approx.

43:**45**:47:**47**:49cm (17:**17¾**:18½:**18½**:19¼in), ending with RS facing.

Cast (bind) off.

FINISHING

Press/block all garment pieces.

Join left shoulder seam.

Neckband

Using 4mm (US size 6) needles and C, re-join yarn and k 31(**31**:35:**35**:37) sts left on a holder at back neck, pick up and k 11 sts down left front neck, re-join yarn to 13(**13**:17:**17**:19) sts left on a holder at front neck, and then pick up and k 11 sts up right front neck. *66(66:74:74:78) sts*

Next row (WS): P2, *k2, p2; rep from * to end.

Next row: K2, *p2, k2; rep from * to end.

These last 2 rows form rib.

Cont in rib until neckband measures approx. 3.5cm (1½in), ending with RS facing.

Cast (bind) off in rib.

Join right shoulder and neckband seam.

Join centre of sleeve cast (bind) off to shoulder seam and sew sleeve approx. 18:**18**:20:**20**:22cm (7:**7**:8:**8**:8¾in) down each side of shoulder seam.

Join side and sleeve seam; rep for second sleeve.

Press/block again if needed.

STRIPE ALTERNATIVES

Option two – wider even stripes

Change to A.

Row 1 (RS): K.

Row 2: P.

Work these 2 rows once more.

Change to B

Row 5 (RS): K.

Row 6: P.

Work these 2 rows once more.

These 8 rows rep form stripe option two.

Option three – introducing a third colour

Change to A.

Row 1 (RS): K.

Row 2: P.

Work these 2 rows once more.

Change to C.

Row 5 (RS): K.

Row 6: P.

Change to A.

Row 7 (RS): K.

Row 8: P.

Work these 2 rows once more.

Change to B.

Row 11 (RS): K.

Row 12: P.

Work these 2 rows once more.

These 12 rows rep form stripe option three.

HINTS AND TIPS

▶ Using your chosen colour palette, swatch different colour options before starting your project – this doesn't need to be the colours used in the project here, they can be any of your choice.

⊙ Use as many or as few colours for your stripe sequence as you like!

◗ If you're feeling adventurous you could try a different stripe sequence for the sleeves than that on the garment body.

Set-in

This section is all about the shaping of the armhole on the body and fitting the sleeve into it. The set-in style is such a flattering and classic fit – it suits everyone and is actually much easier to achieve than you might think. It's all about casting (binding) off and decreasing in the right places.

Primrose on page 98 has to be my favourite project from the set-in section. Adding a tie to the waist of a garment creates a completely different silhouette; it takes this garment from relaxed to fitted. You could also try adding a tie to the cuffs instead of the waist, or to a different project within the book.

As well as working with ties, this section covers adding a striped sleeve, personalizing your knits with brooches, contrast fairisle and working a cabled cuff. Just as in the square section, all the bodies and sleeves of the garments in the set-in section can be mixed and matched – and again you can play with different yarn weights, colours and stripes.

LILY

[SET-IN | Striped Sleeve Sweater]

FREESIA

[SET-IN | Cable Cuffs]

JASMINE

[SET-IN | Personalize Cable Sweater]

PAGES 98–103

PRIMOSE

[SET-IN | Tie Sweater]

ISLA

[SET-IN | Contrast Fairisle Sweater]

LILY

[SET-IN | Striped Sleeve Sweater]

A strong sleeve detail always inspires me; I love the idea of a fun and unique sleeve. You can add a striped sleeve to any project within this book – even the cable sleeves on the Magnolia (see page 36) and Jasmine (see page 95) sweaters.

TECHNIQUE
Adding striped sleeves

SIZE Note sizes are approximate.

	Small	Medium	Large	X Large	XX Large	
To fit	81–86	91–96	101–106	112–117	122–127	cm
	32–34	36–38	40–42	44–46	48–50	in
Actual	118	130	140	150	162	cm
(approx.)	46½	51¼	55	59	63¾	in
Length	60	61	62	64	68	cm
(approx.)	23½	24	24½	25¼	26¾	in
Sleeve seam	43	45	47	47	49	cm
(approx.)	17	17¾	18½	18½	19¼	in

YARN
DK (light worsted)
Sample made in
KPC Gossyp DK
(100% Organic Cotton, approx.
113m/123yd per 50g/1¾oz ball)
4(**5**:6:**7**:8) balls of Ballerina (**A**)
6(**7**:8:**9**:10) balls of Black Ice (**B**)
3(**3**:4:**4**:5) balls of Inca (**C**)
3(**3**:4:**4**:5) balls of Optic White (**D**)
3(**3**:4:**4**:5) balls of Black (**E**)

NEEDLES AND OTHER ITEMS
4mm (US size 6) knitting needles
Cable needle
2 stitch holders

TENSION (GAUGE)
22 sts x 28 rows = 10cm (4in) square
working st st on 4mm (US size 6) needles.

ABBREVIATIONS
See page 20

SPECIAL ABBREVIATIONS
C4B (cable 4 back): slip next 2 sts onto
a cable needle and hold at back of work,
k next 2 sts from left-hand needle and
then k 2 sts from cable needle
MB (make bobble): (k1, yf, k1, yf, k1) all
into next st, turn, p5, turn, k5, turn, p2tog,
p1, p2tog, turn, slip 1 st, k2tog, psso over
(bobble complete)
T3B (twist 3 back): slip next st onto cable
needle and hold at back of work, k next
2 sts from left-hand needle, then p st
from cable needle
T3F (twist 3 front): slip next 2 sts onto
cable needle and hold at front of work,
p next st from left-hand needle, then
k 2 sts from cable needle
T5R (twist 5 right): slip next 3 sts onto
cable needle and hold at back of work,
knit next 2 sts from left-hand needle,
then work (p1, k2) from cable needle

MAKE

BACK

Using 4mm (US size 6) needles and A,
cast on 130(**142**:154:**166**:178) sts.
Now work in rib as folls:

Row 1 (RS): *K2, p2; rep from * to last 2 sts, k2.
Row 2: *P2, k2; rep from * to last 2 sts, p2.
These 2 rows rep form rib.
Cont in rib until work measures approx. 4cm
(1⅝in) from cast-on edge, ending with RS facing.
Now work in st st as folls:

Row 1 (RS): K.
Row 2: P.
These 2 rows rep form st st.
Cont in st st until work measures approx. 21cm
(8¼in) from cast-on edge, ending with **WS** facing.
Change to B.
Next row (WS): P2tog, p to end.
*129(**141**:153:**165**:177) sts*
Now set cable placement as folls:

Set up row 1 (RS): P16, k4, p4, k2, [p4, k4] twice,
p4, k2, p4, k4, p6, k5, p6, k4, p4, k2, [p4, k4] twice,
p4, k2, p4, k4, p16.
Set up row 2: K16, p4, k4, p2, [k4, p4] twice, k4,
p2, k4, p4, k6, p5, k6, p4, k4, p2, [k4, p4] twice, k4,
p2, k4, p4, k16.
Row 1: P16, C4B, p4, k2, p4, C4B, p4, C4B, p4, k2,
p4, C4B, p6, T5R, p6, C4B, p4, k2, p4, C4B, p4, C4B,
p4, k2, p4, C4B, p16.
Row 2: K16, p4, k4, p2, [k4, p4] twice, k4, p2, k4,
p4, k6, p2, k1, p2, k6, p4, k4, p2, [k4, p4] twice, k4,
p2, k4, p4, k16.
Row 3: P16, k4, p4, k2, [p4, k4] twice, p4, k2, p4,
k4, p5, T3B, p1, T3F, p5, k4, p4, k2, [p4, k4] twice,
p4, k2, p4, k4, p16.
Row 4: K16, p4, k4, p2, [k4, p4] twice, k4, p2, k4,
p4, k5, p2, k3, p2, k5, p4, k4, p2, [k4, p4] twice, k4,
p2, k4, p4, k16.

Row 5: P16, C4B, p4, k2, p4, C4B, p4, C4B, p4, k2,
p4, C4B, p4, T3B, p3, T3F, p4, C4B, p4, k2, p4, C4B,
p4, C4B, p4, k2, p4, C4B, p16.
Row 6: K16, p4, k4, p2, [k4, p4] twice, k4, p2, k4,
p4, k4, p2, k5, p2, k4, p4, k4, p2, [k4, p4] twice, k4,
p2, k4, p4, k16.
Row 7: P16, k4, p4, k2, [p4, k4] twice, p4, k2, p4, k4,
p4, k2, p2, MB, p2, k2, p4, k4, p4, k2, [p4, k4] twice,
p4, k2, p4, k4, p16.
Row 8: As Row 6.
Row 9: P16, C4B, p4, k2, p4, [C4B, p4] twice, k2, p4,
C4B, p4, T3F, p3, T3B, p4, C4B, p4, k2, p4, [p4, C4B]
twice, p4, k2, p4, C4B, p16.
Row 10: As Row 4.
Row 11: P16, k4, p4, k2, [p4, k4] twice, p4, k2, p4,
k4, p5, T3F, p1, T3B, p5, k4, p4, k2, [p4, k4] twice,
p4, k2, p4, k4, p16.
Row 12: As Row 2.
These 12 rows rep form cable patt.
Cont as set until work measures approx. 36cm
(14in), ending with RS facing.

Armhole shaping

Keep cable placement correct throughout.
Cast (bind) off 4 sts at beg of next 2 rows.
*121(**133**:145:**157**:169) sts*
Cast (bind) off 2 sts at beg of next 2 rows.
*117(**129**:141:**153**:165) sts*
Next 2 rows: Ssk, k to last 2 sts, k2tog.
*113(**125**:137:**149**:161) sts*
Now cont straight keeping cable patt correct
until work measures approx. 43cm (17in) from
cast-on edge, ending with RS facing.
Change to C.**
Now work in st st only until armhole measures
approx. 18:**19**:20:**22**:24cm (7:**7½**:8:**8¾**:9½in) from
beg of armhole shaping, ending with RS facing.

Shoulder shaping

Cast (bind) off 12(**14**:16:**17**:19) sts at beg of
next 4 rows. *65(**69**:73:**81**:85) sts*
Cast (bind) off 13(**15**:17:**19**:21) sts at beg of
next 2 rows. *39(**39**:39:**43**:43) sts*
Leave rem 39(**39**:39:**43**:43) sts on a holder
at back neck.

FRONT

Work as for Back to **.
Now work straight in st st until armhole measures
approx. 12:**12**:14:**14**:16cm (4¾:**4¾**:5½:**5½**:6¼in) from
beg of armhole shaping, ending with RS facing.

Front neck shaping

With RS facing and keeping st st correct
throughout, work over next 50(**56**:62:**66**:72) sts,
turn work, leaving all rem sts on a st holder.

Left front neck

Next row (WS): Cast (bind) off 8 sts, p to end.
*42(**48**:54:**58**:64) sts*
Work RS row.
Next row (WS): Cast (bind) off 3 sts, p to end.
*39(**45**:51:**55**:61) sts*
Work RS row.
Next row (WS): Cast (bind) off 2 sts, p to end.
*37(**43**:49:**53**:59) sts*
Now work straight in st st until armhole measures
approx. 18:**18**:20:**20**:22cm (7:**7**:8:**8**:8¾in) from beg
of armhole shaping, ending with RS facing.

Left shoulder shaping

Next row (RS): Cast (bind) off 12(**14**:16:**17**:19) sts,
k to end. *25(**29**:33:**36**:40) sts*
Work **WS** row.
Next row (RS): Cast (bind) off 12(**14**:16:**17**:19) sts,
k to end. *13(**15**:17:**19**:21) sts*
Work **WS** row.
Cast (bind) off rem 13(**15**:17:**19**:21) sts.

Centre and right front neck

With RS facing, keep centre 13(**13**:13:**17**:17) sts
at front neck on a holder and work on rem
50(**56**:62:**66**:72) sts as folls:
Next row (RS): Cast (bind) off 8 sts, k to end.
*42(**48**:54:**58**:64) sts*
Work **WS** row.
Next row (RS): Cast (bind) off 3 sts, k to end.
*39(**45**:51:**55**:61) sts*
Work **WS** row.
Next row (RS): Cast (bind) off 2 sts, k to end.
*37(**43**:49:**53**:59) sts*
Now work straight in st st until armhole measures
approx. 18:**18**:20:**20**:22cm (7:**7**:8:**8**:8¾in) from beg of
armhole shaping, ending with **WS** facing.

Right shoulder shaping

Next row (WS): Cast (bind) off 12(**14**:16:**17**:19) sts,
p to end. *25(**29**:33:**36**:40) sts*
Work RS row.
Next row (WS): Cast (bind) off 12(**14**:16:**17**:19) sts,
p to end. *13(**15**:17:**19**:21) sts*
Work RS row.
Cast (bind) off rem 13(**15**:17:**19**:21) sts.

SLEEVES (make 2)

Using 4mm (US 7) knitting needles and D,
cast on 34(**38**:42:**42**:46) sts.
Now work in rib as folls:
Row 1 (RS): *K2, p2; rep from * to last 2 sts, k2.
Row 2: *P2, k2; rep from * to last 2 sts, p2.
These 2 rows rep form rib.
Cont in rib until work measures approx. 4cm
(1⅝in) from cast-on edge, ending with RS facing.
Now work in striped st st as folls:
Row 1 (RS): K.
Row 2: P.
Change to E.

Row 3: K.

Row 4: P.

Change to D.

These 4 rows rep (including yarn changes) form striped st st.

Cont in striped st st as set WHILST AT THE SAME TIME inc 1 st at each end of every sixth row to 58(**62**:66:**66**:70) sts, ending with RS facing.

Cont straight in striped st st until work measures approx. 43:**45**:47:**47**:49cm (17:**17¾**:18½:**18½**:19¼in), ending with RS facing.

Armhole shaping

Keep striped st st correct throughout.

Cast (bind) off 4 sts at beg of next 2 rows. *50(**54**:58:**58**:62) sts*

Cast (bind) off 2 sts at beg of next 2 rows. *46(**50**:54:**54**:58) sts*

Next row (RS): Ssk, k to last 2 sts, k2tog. *44(**48**:52:**52**:56) sts*

Work **WS** row.

Next row (RS): Ssk, k to last 2 sts, k2tog. *42(**46**:50:**50**:54) sts*

Next row (WS): P2tog, p to last 2 sts, p2tog. *40(**44**:48:**48**:52) sts*

Work 4 rows straight in striped st st.

Next row (RS): Ssk, k to last 2 sts, k2tog. *38(**42**:46:**46**:50) sts*

Work **WS** row.

Rep last 2 rows five times more. *28(**32**:36:**36**:40) sts*

Next row (RS): Ssk, k to last 2 sts, k2tog. *26(**30**:34:**34**:38) sts*

Work **WS** row.

Next row (RS): Ssk, k to last 2 sts, k2tog. *24(**28**:32:**32**:36) sts*

Rep last row once more. *22(**26**:30:**30**:34) sts*

Cast (bind) off 2 sts at beg of next 6 rows. *10(**14**:18:**18**:22) sts*

Cast (bind) off.

FINISHING

Press/block all garment pieces.

Join left shoulder seam.

Neckband

Using 4mm (US 7) knitting needles and with RS facing, re-join yarn C to 39(**39**:39:**43**:43) sts left on a holder at back neck, pick up and k 19(**21**:21:**23**:23) sts down left front neck, re-join yarn to 13(**13**:13:**17**:17) sts at front neck, and then pick up and k 19(**21**:21:**23**:23) sts up right front neck. *90(**94**:94:**106**:106) sts*

Next row (WS): *P2, k2; rep from * to last 2 sts, p2.

Now work in rib as folls:

Row 1 (RS): *K2, p2; rep from * to last 2 sts, k2.

Row 2: *P2, k2; rep from * to last 2 sts, p2.

These 2 rows rep form rib, rep them until rib measures approx. 8cm (3⅛in), ending with RS facing. Cast (bind) off in rib.

Join right shoulder and neckband seam.

Fold rib back (so neckband is doubled) and sew down on inside edge of neckband.

Join centre of sleeve head cast (bind) off to shoulder seam and ease sleeve into armhole of garment body; rep for second sleeve. Join side and sleeve seams.

Press/block again if needed.

HINTS AND TIPS

▶ Work whatever stripe sequence you like for the sleeve; you could even try introducing a third colour.

⦿ When choosing yarn for this project the key is to pick a yarn for the central cable panel with some texture; this could be through colour or fibre.

FREESIA

[SET-IN | Cable Cuffs]

Adding a horizontal cable instead of a classic ribbed or garter cuff will create such a beautiful finished sleeve. You can add pretty much any cable you like; just knit the cuff to the correct length and make sure you pick up the right number of stitches to begin your sleeve.

TECHNIQUE
Cable cuffs

SIZE Note sizes are approximate.

	Small	Medium	Large	X Large	XX Large	
To fit	81–86	91–96	101–106	112–117	122–127	cm
	32–34	36–38	40–42	44–46	48–50	in
Actual	122	130	144	150	158	cm
(approx.)	48	51¼	56¾	59	62	in
Length	52	54	56	58	60	cm
(approx.)	20½	21¼	22	23	23½	in
Sleeve seam	32	32	34	36	38	cm
(approx.)	12½	12½	13½	14	15	in

YARN
DK (light worsted)
Sample made in
Erika Knight British Blue 100
(80% Wool, approx. 220m/241yd
per 100g/3½oz hank)
5(**6**:6:**7**:8) hanks of Cymbeline

NEEDLES AND OTHER ITEMS
4mm (US size 6) knitting needles
Cable needle
2 stitch holders

TENSION (GAUGE)
22 sts x 30 rows = 10cm (4in) square
working st st on 4mm (US size 6) needles.
25 sts x 40 rows = 10cm (4in) square
working linen st on 4mm (US size 6)
needles.

ABBREVIATIONS
See page 20

SPECIAL ABBREVIATIONS
C6B (cable 6 back): slip next 3 sts onto
a cable needle and hold at back of work,
k next 3 sts from left-hand needle and
then k 3 sts from cable needle
C5F (cable 5 front): slip next 2 sts onto
a cable needle and hold at front of work,
k next 3 sts from left-hand needle and
then k 2 sts from cable needle.
C6F (cable 6 front): slip next 3 sts onto
a cable needle and hold at front of work,
k next 3 sts from left-hand needle and
then k 3 sts from cable needle
T3B (twist 3 back): slip next st onto cable
needle and hold at back of work, k next
2 sts from left-hand needle, then p st
from cable needle
T3F (twist 3 front): slip next 2 sts onto
cable needle and hold at front of work,
p next st from left-hand needle, then
k 2 sts from cable needle

CABLES

DIAMOND CABLE (21 sts)
Row 1 (RS): P8, C5F, p8.
Row 2: K8, p2, k1, p2, k8.
Row 3: P7, T3B, k1, T3F, p7.
Row 4: K7, p2, k1, p1, k1, p2, k7.
Row 5: P6, T3B, k1, p1, k1, T3F, p6.
Row 6: K6, p2, [k1, p1] twice, k1, p2, k6.
Row 7: P5, T3B, [k1, p1] twice, k1, T3F, p5.
Row 8: K5, p2, [k1, p1] three times, k1, p2, k5.
Row 9: P4, T3B, [k1, p1] three times, k1, T3F, p4.
Row 10: K4, p2, [k1, p1] four times, k1, p2, k4.
Row 11: P4, T3F, [p1, k1] three times, p1, T3B, p4.
Row 12: K5, p2, [k1, p1] three times, k1, p2, k5.
Row 13: P5, T3F, [p1, k1] twice, p1, T3B, p5.
Row 14: K6, p2, [k1, p1] twice, k1, p2, k6.
Row 15: P6, T3F, p1, k1, p1, T3B, p6.
Row 16: K7, p2, k1, p1, k1, p2, k7.
Row 17: P7, T3F, p1, T3B, p7.
Row 18: K8, p2, k1, p2, k8.
These 18 rows rep form Diamond Cable,
work when stated in patt.

WAVE CABLE (20 sts)
Row 1 (RS): P7, k2, p2, k2, p7.
Row 2: K7, p2, k2, p2, k7.
Row 3: P6, T3B, p2, T3F, p6.
Row 4: K6, p2, k4, p2, k6.
Row 5: P5, T3B, p4, T3F, p5.
Row 6: K5, p2, k6, p2, k5.
Row 7: P4, T3B, p6, T3F, p4.
Row 8: K4, p2, k8, p2, k4.
Row 9: P4, k2, p8, k2, p4.
Row 10: K4, p2, k8, p2, k4.
Row 11: P4, T3F, p6, T3B, p4.
Row 12: K5, p2, k6, p2, k5.
Row 13: P5, T3F, p4, T3B, p5.
Row 14: K6, p2, k4, p2, k6.
Row 15: P6, T3F, p2, T3B, p6.
Row 16: K7, p2, k2, p2, k7.
These 16 rows rep form Wave Cable,
work when stated in patt.

MAKE

BACK
Using 4mm (US size 6) needles, cast on
134(**142**:158:**166**:174) sts.

Row 1 (RS): [K2, p2] 10(**11**:13:**14**:15) times, k2, p3,
k4, p3, [k2, p2] 7 times, k2, p3, k4, p3, [k2, p2]
10(**11**:13:**14**:15) times, k2.

Row 2: [P2, k2] 10(**11**:13:**14**:15) times, p2, k3, p4, k3,
[p2, k2] 7 times, p2, k3, p4, k3, [p2, k2] 10(**11**:13:**14**:15)
times, p2.

These 2 rows rep form rib.

Cont in rib until work measures approx. 2.5cm (1in),
ending with **WS** facing.

Next row: K36(**40**:48:**52**:56), p2, k2, M1, k5, p2, M1,
p2, k5, M1, k2, p2, k2, M1, k4, p2, k2, p2, k4, M1, k2, p2,
k2, M1, k5, p2, M1, p2, k5, M1, k2, p2, k36(**40**:48:**52**:56).
*142(**150**:166:**174**:182) sts*

Now work cable and rib patt as folls:

Row 1 (RS): P36(**40**:44:**52**:56), k2, work 21 sts of
Diamond Cable Row 1, k2, work 20 sts of Wave
Cable Row 1, k2, work 21 sts of Diamond Cable
Row 1, k2, p36(**40**:44:**52**:56).

Row 2: K36(**40**:44:**52**:56), p2, work 21 sts of Diamond
Cable Row 2, p2, work 20 sts of Wave Cable Row
2, p2, work 21 sts of Diamond Cable Row 2, p2,
k36(**40**:44:**52**:56).

Row 3: P36(**40**:44:**52**:56), k2, work 21 sts of Diamond
Cable Row 3, k2, work 20 sts of Wave Cable Row
3, k2, work 21 sts of Diamond Cable Row 3, k2,
p36(**40**:44:**52**:56).

Row 4: K36(**40**:44:**52**:56), p2, work 21 sts of Diamond
Cable Row 4, p2, work 20 sts of Wave Cable Row
4, p2, work 21 sts of Diamond Cable Row 4, p2,
k36(**40**:44:**52**:56).

These 4 rows set Diamond and Wave Cable and
rib placement on rev st st background.

Cont as set, working all 18 rows of Diamond
Cable and 16 rows of Wave Cable (please note:

these will not end on the same placement row)
until work measures approx. 34(**36**:36:**38**:38:cm
(13½:**14**:14:**15**:15in) from cast-on edge, ending
with RS facing.

Armhole shaping
Keep cable placement correct throughout.
Cast (bind) off 8 sts at beg of next 2 rows.
*126(**134**:142:**158**:166) sts*
Cast (bind) off 4 sts at beg of next 2 rows.
*118(**126**:134:**150**:158) sts*
Cast (bind) off 2 sts at beg of next 4 rows.
*110(**118**:126:**142**:150) sts ***

Now cont straight keeping cable placement
correct throughout until armhole measures
approx. 18:**18**:20:**20**:22cm (7:**7**:8:**8**:8¾in) from
beg of armhole shaping, ending with RS facing.

Shoulder shaping
Keep cable placement correct throughout.
Cast (bind) off 33(**37**:40:**47**:50) sts at beg of
next 2 rows. *44(**44**:46:**48**:50) sts*
Leave rem 44(**44**:46:**48**:50) sts on a holder
at back neck.

FRONT
Work as for Back to **.

Now cont straight keeping cable placement
correct throughout until armhole measures
approx. 10:**10**:12:**12**:14cm (4:**4**:4¾:**4¾**:5½in) from
beg of armhole shaping, ending with RS facing.

Front neck shaping
With RS facing and keeping cable placement
correct throughout, work over next 44(**48**:51:**58**:61)
sts, turn work, leaving all rem sts on a st holder.

Left front neck
Next row (WS): Cast (bind) off 6 sts, cable patt
to end. *38(**42**:45:**52**:55) sts*
Work RS row.

Next row (WS): Cast (bind) off 3 sts, cable patt to end. 35(**39**:42:**49**:52) sts
Work RS row.
Next row (WS): Cast (bind) off 2 sts, cable patt to end. 33(**37**:40:**47**:50) sts
Now work straight keeping cable placement correct until armhole measures approx. 18:**18**:20:**20**:22cm (7:**7**:8:**8**:8¾in) from beg of armhole shaping, ending with RS facing.
Cast (bind) off.

Centre and right front neck
With RS facing, keep centre 22(**22**:24:**26**:28) sts at front neck on a holder and work on rem 44(**48**:51:**58**:61) sts as folls:
Next row (RS): Cast (bind) off 6 sts, cable patt to end. 38(**42**:45:**52**:55) sts
Work **WS** row.
Next row (RS): Cast (bind) off 3 sts, cable patt to end. 35(**39**:42:**49**:52) sts
Work **WS** row.
Next row (RS): Cast (bind) off 2 sts, cable patt to end. 33(**37**:40:**47**:50) sts
Now work straight keeping cable placement correct until armhole measures approx. 18:**18**:20:**20**:22cm (7:**7**:8:**8**:8¾in) from beg of armhole shaping, ending with **WS** facing.
Cast (bind) off.

CUFF (make 2)
Using 4mm (US size 6) needles, cast on 16 sts.
Row 1 (RS): K.
Row 2: K2, p to last 2 sts, k2.
Row 3: K2, C6B, C6F, k2.
Row 4: K2, p to last 2 sts, k2.
Rep Rows 1 and 2 once more.
These 6 rows rep form cable with garter st edging.
Cont as set until cuff measures approx.

22:**22**:24:**24**:28cm (8¾:**8¾**:9½:**9½**:11in) from cast-on edge, ending with RS facing and Row 2 or 6 of patt.
Cast (bind) off.

SLEEVES (make 2)
Using 4mm (US size 6) needles, evenly pick up 55(**55**:61:**61**:71) sts across right edge of cuff.
Next row (WS): P.
Now work in linen st as folls:
Row 1 (RS): K1, *yf, sl 1 purlwise, yb, k1; rep from * to end.
Row 2: P.
Row 3: K2, *yf, sl 1 purlwise, yb, k1; rep from * to last st, k1.
Row 4: P.
These 4 rows rep form linen st.
Cont in linen st WHILST AT THE SAME TIME inc 1 st at each end of next and then every sixth row to 81(**81**:85:**85**:95) sts, ending with RS facing.
Cont straight in linen st until work measures approx. 32:**32**:34:**36**:38cm (12½:**12½**:13½:**14**:15in), ending with RS facing.

Armhole shaping
Keep linen st correct throughout.
Cast (bind) off 8 sts at beg of next 2 rows.
65(**65**:69:**69**:79) sts
Cast (bind) off 4 sts at beg of next 2 rows.
57(**57**:61:**61**:71) sts
Cast (bind) off 2 sts at beg of next 4 rows.
49(**49**:53:**53**:63) sts
Dec 1 st at each end of next row. 47(**47**:51:**51**:61) sts
Work 3 rows.
Rep last 4 rows three times more.
41(**41**:45:**45**:55) sts
Dec 1 st at each end of next row.
39(**39**:43:**43**:53) sts
Work **WS** row.

Rep last 2 rows five times more. *29(**29**:33:**33**:43) sts*
Dec 1 st at each end of next 2 rows. *25(**25**:29:**29**:39) sts*
Cast (bind) off 4(**4**:4:**4**:6) sts at beg of next 4 rows.
*9(**9**:13:**13**:15) sts*
Cast (bind) off.

FINISHING
Press/block all garment pieces.
Join left shoulder seam.

Neckband
Using 4mm (US size 6) needles and with RS facing,
re-join yarn and k 44(**44**:46:**48**:50) sts left on a
holder at back neck, pick up and k 22 sts evenly
down left neck, re-join yarn and k 22(**22**:24:**26**:28)
sts left on a holder at front neck, and then
pick up and k 22 sts evenly up right front neck.
*110(**110**:114:**118**:122) sts*
Next row (WS): P2, *k2, p2; rep from * to end.
Next row: K2, *p2, k2; rep from * to end.
These last 2 rows rep form rib.
Cont in rib until neckband measures approx.
2.5cm (1in), ending with RS facing.
Cast (bind) off in rib.
Join right shoulder and neckband seam.
Join centre of sleeve head cast (bind) off to
shoulder seam and ease sleeve into armhole
of garment body; rep for second sleeve. Join
side and sleeve seams.
Press/block again if needed.

HINTS AND TIPS
▶ To pick up the stitches neatly, insert
your needle straight into your work exactly
where you want the stitch to be; use
the knitting almost like you would your
second needle. To pick up a stitch: insert
the needle into the work, wrap the yarn
around the needle and pull the needle
with yarn back up through the work
(1 stitch on the needle). Repeat this until
you have all the stitches on the needle.

⦿ Using the above method of picking
up stitches means you **won't** need to
knit into the back of the picked up stitch
to prevent holes.

JASMINE

[SET-IN | Personalize Cable Sweater]

We all have a stash of brooches or badges hidden somewhere in our wardrobe or trinket box and it's a shame to hide them away. The classic aran look of this garment creates a beautiful blank canvas to pin your hidden treasures on; add as many or as few as you like.

TECHNIQUE
Adding badges or brooches to knitwear

SIZE Note sizes are approximate.

	Small	Medium	Large	X Large	XX Large	
To fit	81–86	91–96	101–106	112–117	122–127	cm
	32–34	36–38	40–42	44–46	48–50	in
Actual	120	130	140	150	160	cm
(approx.)	47¼	51¼	55	59	63	in
Length	54	54	58	60	64	cm
(approx.)	21¼	21¼	23	23½	25¼	in
Sleeve seam	43	45	47	47	49	cm
(approx.)	17	17¾	18½	18½	19¼	in

YARN
Aran (worsted)
Sample made in
Debbie Bliss Donegal Luxury Tweed Aran
(100% Wool, approx. 88m/96yd per
50g/1¾oz ball)
10(**10**:11:**12**:13) balls of Oatmeal

NEEDLES AND OTHER ITEMS
5mm (US size 8) knitting needles
Cable needle
2 stitch holders

TENSION (GAUGE)
18 sts x 24 rows = 10cm (4in) square working
rev st st on 5mm (US size 8) needles.

ABBREVIATIONS
See page 20

SPECIAL ABBREVIATIONS
C6B (cable 6 back): slip next 3 sts onto

a cable needle and hold at back of work,
k next 3 sts from left-hand needle and
then k 3 sts from cable needle
C5B (cable 5 back): slip next 3 sts onto
a cable needle and back at front of work,
k next 2 sts from left-hand needle, then
k 3 sts from cable needle
MB (make bobble): (k1, yf, k1, yf, k1) all
into next st, turn, p5, turn, k5, turn,
p2tog, p1, p2tog, turn, slip 1 st, k2tog,
psso (bobble complete)
T3B (twist 3 back): slip next st onto cable
needle and hold at back of work, k next
2 sts from left-hand needle, then p st
from cable needle
T3F (twist 3 front): slip next 2 sts onto
cable needle and hold at front of work,
p next st from left-hand needle, then
k 2 sts from cable needle

PATTERN NOTE
All cable panels are underlined throughout

MAKE

BACK

Using 5mm (US size 8) needles, cast on
110(**118**:126:**138**:146) sts.

Now work in rib as folls:

Row 1 (RS): *K2, p2; rep from * to last 2 sts, k2.

Row 2: *P2, k2; rep from * to last 2 sts, p2.

These 2 rows rep form rib.

Cont in rib until work measures approx. 3.5cm
(1½in) from cast-on edge, ending with RS facing.

Next row (RS): *K2, p2; rep from * to last 2 sts,
k2tog. *109(**117**:125:**137**:145) sts*

Place cable on rev st st background as folls:

Row 1 (WS): K20(**24**:28:**34**:38), p6, k6, p6, k10,
k4, p2, k1, p2, k4, k10, p6, k6, p6, k20(**24**:28:**34**:38).

Row 2 (RS): P20(**24**:28:**34**:38), C6B, p6, C6B, p10, p3,
T3B, k1, T3F, p3, p10, C6B, p6, C6B, p20(**24**:28:**34**:38).

Row 3: K20(**24**:28:**34**:38), p6, k6, p6, k10, k3, p2, k1, p1,
k1, p2, k3, k10, p6, k6, p6, k20(**24**:28:**34**:38).

Row 4: P20(**24**:28:**34**:38), k6, p6, k6, p10, p2, T3B, k1,
p1, k1, T3F, p2, p10, k6, p6, k6, p20(24:28:**34**:38).

Row 5: K20(**24**:28:**34**:38), p6, k6, p6, k10, k2, p2, [k1,
p1] twice, k1, p2, k2, k10, p6, k6, p6, k20(**24**:28:**34**:38).

Row 6: P20(**24**:28:**34**:38), k6, p6, k6, p10, p1,
T3B, [k1, p1] twice, k1, T3F, p1, p10, k6, p6, k6,
p20(**24**:28:**34**:38).

Row 7: K20(**24**:28:**34**:38), p6, k6, p6, k10, k1, p2,
[k1, p1] three times, k1, p2, k1, k10, p6, k6, p6,
k20(**24**:28:**34**:38).

Row 8: P20(**24**:28:**34**:38), C6B, p6, C6B, p10, T3B,
[k1, p1] three times, k1, T3F, p10, C6B, p6, C6B,
p20(**24**:28:**34**:38).

Row 9: K20(**24**:28:**34**:38), p6, k6, p6, k10, p2, [k1, p1]
four times, k1, p2, k10, p6, k6, p6, k20(**24**:28:**34**:38).

Row 10: P20(**24**:28:**34**:38), k6, p6, k6, p10, T3F,
[p1, k1] three times, p1, T3B, p10, k6, p6, k6,
p20(**24**:28:**34**:38).

Row 11: K20(**24**:28:**34**:38), p6, k6, p6, k10, k1, p2,

[k1, p1] three times, k1, p2, k1, k10, p6, k6, p6,
k20(**24**:28:**34**:38).

Row 12: P20(**24**:28:**34**:38), k6, p6, k6, p10, p1,
T3F, [p1, k1] twice, p1, T3B, p1, p10, k6, p6, k6,
p20(**24**:28:**34**:38).

Row 13: As Row 5.

Row 14: P20(**24**:28:**34**:38), C6B, p6, C6B, p10,
p2, T3F, p1, k1, p1, T3B, p2, p10, C6B, p6, C6B,
p20(**24**:28:**34**:38).

Row 15: As Row 3.

Row 16: P20(**24**:28:**34**:38), k6, p6, k6, p10, p3, T3F, p1,
T3B, p3, p10, k6, p6, k6, p20(**24**:28:**34**:38).

Row 17: As Row 1.

Row 18: P20(**24**:28:**34**:38), k6, p6, k6, p10, p4, C5B, p4,
p10, k6, p6, k6, p20(**24**:28:**34**:38).

Row 19: As Row 1.

Row 20: P20(**24**:28:**34**:38), C6B, p6, C6B, p10, p3,
T3B, p1, T3F, p3, p10, C6B, p6, C6B, p20(**24**:28:**34**:38).

Row 21: K20(**24**:28:**34**:38), p6, k6, p6, k10, [k3, p2]
twice, k3, k10, p6, k6, p6, k20(**24**:28:**34**:38).

Row 22: P20(**24**:28:**34**:38), k6, p6, k6, p10, p2, T3B, p3,
T3F, p2, p10, k6, p6, k6, p20(**24**:28:**34**:38).

Row 23: K20(**24**:28:**34**:38), p6, k6, p6, k10, k2, p2, k5,
p2, k2, k10, p6, k6, p6, k20(**24**:28:**34**:38).

Row 24: P20(**24**:28:**34**:38), k6, p6, k6, p10, p2, k2, p2,
MB, p2, k2, p2, p10, k6, p6, k6, p20(**24**:28:**34**:38).

Row 25: As Row 23.

Row 26: P20(**24**:28:**34**:38), C6B, p6, C6B, p10, p2, T3F,
p3, T3B, p2, p10, C6B, p6, C6B, p20(**24**:28:**34**:38).

Row 27: As Row 21.

Row 28: P20(**24**:28:**34**:38), k6, p6, k6, p10, p3, T3F, p1,
T3B, p3, p10, k6, p6, k6, p20(**24**:28:**34**:38).

Row 29: As Row 1.

Row 30: As Row 18.

These 30 rows set cable placement on rev st st.
Cont as set keeping cable placement on rev st st
correct throughout.

Cast (bind) off 4 sts at beg of next 2 rows.
101(109:117:129:137) sts
Cast (bind) off 2 sts at beg of next 2 rows.
97(105:113:125:133) sts
Next 2 rows: Ssk, patt to last 2 sts, k2tog.
*93(101:109:121:129) sts **
Now work straight in cable patt until armhole
measures approx. 18:**18**:20:**20**:22cm (7:**7**:8:**8**:8¾in)
from beg of armhole shaping, ending with RS
facing.

Shoulder shaping
Cast (bind) off 10(**11**:12:**14**:15) sts at beg of next
4 rows. *53(**57**:61:**65**:69) sts*
Cast (bind) off 11(**13**:14:**15**:17) sts at beg of next
2 rows. *31(**31**:33:**35**:35) sts*
Leave rem 31(**31**:33:**35**:35) sts on a holder at
back neck.

FRONT
Work as for Back to **.
Keep cable placement correct throughout.
Now work straight in cable patt until
armhole measures approx. 12:**12**:14:**14**:16cm
(4¾:**4¾**:5½:**5½**:6¼in) from beg of armhole
shaping, ending with RS facing.

Front neck shaping
With RS facing and keeping cable placement
correct throughout work over next 40(**44**:47:**52**:56)
sts, turn work leaving all rem sts on a st holder.

Left front neck
Next row (WS): Cast (bind) off 6 sts, patt to end.
*34(**38**:41:**46**:50) sts*
Work RS row.
Next row (WS): Cast (bind) off 2 sts, patt to end.
*32(**36**:39:**44**:48) sts*
Work RS row.
Next row (WS): K2tog, patt to end.

*31(**35**:38:**43**:47) sts*
Now work straight keeping cable placement
correct until armhole measures approx.
18:**18**:20:**20**:22cm (7:**7**:8:**8**:8¾in) from beg of armhole
shaping, ending with RS facing.

Left shoulder shaping
Next row (RS): Cast (bind) off 10(**11**:12:**14**:15) sts,
patt to end. *21(**24**:26:**29**:32) sts*
Work **WS** row.
Next row (RS): Cast (bind) off 10(**11**:12:**14**:15) sts,
patt to end. *11(**13**:14:**15**:17) sts*
Work **WS** row.
Cast (bind) off rem 11(**13**:14:**15**:17) sts.

Centre and right front neck
With RS facing, keep centre 13(**13**:15:**17**:17) sts
at front neck on a holder and work on rem
40(**44**:47:**52**:56) sts as folls:
Next row (RS): Cast (bind) off 6 sts, patt to end.
*34(**38**:41:**46**:50) sts*
Work **WS** row.
Next row (RS): Cast (bind) off 2 sts, patt to end.
*32(**36**:39:**44**:48) sts*
Work **WS** row.
Next row (RS): K2tog, k to end. *31(**35**:38:**43**:47) sts*
Now work straight keeping cable placement
correct until armhole measures approx.
18:**18**:20:**20**:22cm (7:**7**:8:**8**:8¾in) from beg of armhole
shaping, ending with **WS** facing.

Right shoulder shaping
Next row (WS): Cast (bind) off 10(**11**:12:**14**:15) sts,
patt to end. *21(**24**:26:**29**:32) sts*
Work RS row.
Next row (WS): Cast (bind) off 10(**11**:12:**14**:15) sts,
patt to end. *11(**13**:14:**15**:17) sts*
Work RS row.
Cast (bind) off rem 11(**13**:14:**15**:17) sts.

SLEEVES (make 2)

Using 5mm (US size 8) needles, cast on 34(**38**:42:**42**:46) sts.

Now work in rib as folls:

Row 1 (RS): *K2, p2; rep from * to last 2 sts, k2.

Row 2: *P2, k2; rep from * to last 2 sts, p2.

These 2 rows rep form rib.

Cont in rib until work measures approx. 3.5cm (1½in) from cast-on edge, ending with RS facing.

Next row (RS): *K2, p2; rep from * to last 2 sts, k2tog. *33(**37**:41:**41**:45) sts*

Now place cable as folls:

Row 1 (WS): K10(**12**:14:**14**:16), k4, p2, k1, p2, k4, k10(**12**:14:**14**:16).

Row 2 (RS): P10(**12**:14:**14**:16), p3, T3B, k1, T3F, p3, p10(**12**:14:**14**:16).

Row 3: K10(**12**:14:**14**:16), k3, p2, k1, p1, k1, p2, k3, k10(**12**:14:**14**:16).

Row 4: P10(**12**:14:**14**:16), p2, T3B, k1, p1, k1, T3F, p2, p10(**12**:14:**14**:16).

Row 5: K10(**12**:14:**14**:16), k2, p2, [k1, p1] twice, k1, p2, k2, k10(**12**:14:**14**:16).

Row 6 (inc): P1, M1p, p9(**11**:13:**13**:15), p1, T3B, [k1, p1] twice, k1, T3F, p1, p9(**11**:13:**13**:15), M1p, p1. *35(**39**:43:**43**:47) sts*

Row 7: K11(**13**:15:**15**:17), k1, p2, [k1, p1] three times, k1, p2, k1, k11(**13**:15:**15**:17).

Row 8: P11(**13**:15:**15**:17), T3B, [k1, p1] three times, k1, T3F, p11(**13**:15:**15**:17).

Row 9: K11(**13**:15:**15**:17), p2, [k1, p1] four times, k1, p2, k11(**13**:15:**15**:17).

Row 10: P11(**13**:15:**15**:17), T3F, [p1, k1] three times, p1, T3B, p11(**13**:15:**15**:17).

Row 11: K11(**13**:15:**15**:17), k1, p2, [k1, p1] three times, k1, p2, k1, k11(**13**:15:**15**:17).

Row 12 (inc): P1, M1p, p10(**12**:14:**14**:16), p1, T3F, [p1, k1] twice, p1, T3B, p1, M1p, p1. *37(**41**:45:**45**:49) sts*

Row 13: K12(**14**:16:**16**:18), k2, p2, [k1, p1] twice, k1, p2, k2, k12(**14**:16:**16**:18).

Row 14: P12(**14**:16:**16**:18), p2, T3F, p1, k1, p1, T3B, p2, p12(**14**:16:**16**:18).

Row 15: K12(**14**:16:**16**:18), k3, p2, k1, p1, k1, p2, k3, k12(**14**:16:**16**:18).

Row 16: P12(**14**:16:**16**:18), p3, T3F, p1, T3B, p3, p12(**14**:16:**16**:18).

Row 17: K12(**14**:16:**16**:18), k4, p2, k1, p2, k4, k12(**14**:16:**16**:18).

Row 18 (RS): P1, M1p, p11(**13**:15:**15**:17), p4, C5B, p4, p11(**13**:15:**15**:17), M1p, p1. *39(**43**:47:**47**:51) sts*

Row 19: K13(**15**:17:**17**:19), k4, p2, k1, p2, k4, k13(**15**:17:**17**:19).

Row 20: P13(**15**:17:**17**:19), p3, T3B, p1, T3F, p3, p13(**15**:17:**17**:19).

Row 21: K13(**15**:17:**17**:19), [k3, p2] twice, k3, k13(**15**:17:**17**:19).

Row 22: P13(**15**:17:**17**:19), p2, T3B, p3, T3F, p2, p13(**15**:17:**17**:19).

Row 23: K13(**15**:17:**17**:19), k2, p2, k5, p2, k2, k13(**15**:17:**17**:19).

Row 24 (inc): P1, M1p, p12(**14**:16:**16**:18), p2, k2, p2, MB, p2, k2, p2, p12(**14**:16:**16**:18), M1p, p1. *41(**45**:49:**49**:53) sts*

Row 25: K14(**16**:18:**18**:20), k2, p2, k5, p2, k2, k14(**16**:18:**18**:20).

Row 26: P14(**16**:18:**18**:20), p2, T3F, p3, T3B, p2, p14(**16**:18:**18**:20).

Row 27: K14(**16**:18:**18**:20), [k3, p2] twice, k3, k14(**16**:18:**18**:20).

Row 28: P14(**16**:18:**18**:20), p3, T3F, p1, T3B, p3, p14(**16**:18:**18**:20).

Row 29: K14(**16**:18:**18**:20), p4, C5B, p4, k14(**16**:18:**18**:20).

Row 30 (inc): P1, M1p, p13(**15**:17:**17**:19), k4, p2, k1, p2, k4, p13(**15**:17:**17**:19), M1p, p1. *43(**47**:51:**51**:55) sts*

These 30 rows rep form cable placement on rev st st.

Cont as set keeping cable placement on rev st st correct WHILST AT THE SAME TIME inc 1 st at each end of every sixth row (as set) to 57(**61**:65:**65**:69) sts, ending with WS facing.
Cont straight keeping cable placement on rev st st correct until work measures approx. 43(**45**:47:**47**:49cm (17:**17¾**:18½:**18½**:19¼in), ending with RS facing.

Armhole shaping
Keep cable placement correct throughout.
Cast (bind) off 4 sts at beg of next 2 rows. *49(**53**:57:**57**:61) sts*
Cast (bind) off 2 sts at beg of next 2 rows. *45(**49**:53:**53**:57) sts*
Next row (RS): Ssk, patt to last 2 sts, k2tog. *43(**47**:51:**51**:55) sts*
Rep last row twice more, ending with **WS** facing. *39(**43**:47:**47**:51) sts*
Work 3 rows straight keeping cable placement on rev st st correct, ending with RS facing.
Next row (RS): Ssk, patt to last 2 sts, k2tog. *37(**41**:45:**45**:49) sts*
Work **WS** row in patt.
Rep last 2 rows five times more. *27(**31**:35:**35**:39) sts*
Next row (RS): Ssk, patt to last 2 sts, k2tog. *25(**29**:33:**33**:37) sts*
Rep last row three times more ending with RS facing. *19(**23**:27:**27**:31) sts*
Cast (bind) off 2 sts at beg of next 6 rows. *7(**11**:15:**15**:19) sts*
Cast (bind) off.

FINISHING
Press/block all garment pieces.
Join left shoulder seam.

Neckband
Using 5mm (US size 8) needles and with RS facing, re-join yarn to 31(**31**:33:**35**:35) sts left on holder at back neck, pick up and k 19(**21**:21:**23**:23) sts down left front neck, re-join yarn to 13(**13**:15:**17**:17) sts at front neck, and then pick up and k 19(**21**:21:**23**:23) sts up right front neck. *82(**86**:90:**98**:98) sts*
Next row (WS): *P2, k2; rep from * to last 2 sts, p2.
Now work in rib as folls:
Row 1 (RS): *K2, p2; rep from * to last 2 sts, k2.
Row 2: *P2, k2; rep from * to last 2 sts, p2.
These 2 rows rep form rib.
Cont until rib measures approx. 3.5cm (1½in), ending with RS facing.
Cast (bind) off in rib.
Join right shoulder and neckband seam.
Join centre of sleeve head cast (bind) off to shoulder seam and ease sleeve into armhole of garment body; rep for second sleeve. Join side and sleeve seams.
Press/block again if needed.

HINTS AND TIPS
▶ Add as many or as few brooches as you like but stick to odd numbers – odd numbers are always easier on the eye!

◉ If badges are more your thing you can sew them on, or use press studs (snap fasteners).

PRIMROSE

[SET-IN | Tie Sweater]

Adding a tie to your knitwear is a great way to personalize any project; you can do this on any pattern within the book. Why not try it making a thicker or thinner tie for your project – or even working shorter lengths to add ties to the garment cuffs.

TECHNIQUE
Adding ties in knitwear

SIZE Note sizes are approximate.

	Small	Medium	Large	X Large	XX Large	
To fit	81–86	91–96	101–106	112–117	122–127	cm
	32–34	36–38	40–42	44–46	48–50	in
Actual	120	130	140	150	160	cm
(approx.)	47¼	51¼	55	59	63	in
Length	54	54	58	60	64	cm
(approx.)	21¼	21¼	23	23½	25¼	in
Sleeve seam	38	38	40	42	44	cm
(approx.)	15	15	15¾	16½	17¼	in

YARN
Chunky (bulky)
Sample made in
Rowan Cocoon
(80% Wool, 20% Mohair, approx.
115m/126yd per 100g/3½oz ball)
8(**9**:9:**10**:11) balls of Seascape

NEEDLES AND OTHER ITEMS
7mm (US size 10½) knitting needles
2 stitch holders

TENSION (GAUGE)
14 sts x 16 rows = 10cm (4in) square
working st st on 7mm (US size 10½)
needles.

ABBREVIATIONS
See page 20

MAKE

BACK

Using 7mm (US size 10½) needles and thumb method, cast on 84(**92**:98:**106**:112) sts.

Row 1 (WS): P.

Row 2: K.

Work Row 1 once more, ending with RS facing.

Now work in rib as folls:

Rib row 1 (RS): *K1, p1; rep from * to end.

Rib Row 1 ONLY rep forms rib.

Cont in rib until work measures 5cm (2in) from cast-on edge, ending with RS facing.

Now work in st st as folls:

Row 1 (RS): K.

Row 2: P.

These 2 rows rep form st st.

Cont in st st until work measures approx. 36:**36**:38:**40**:42cm (14:**14**:15:**15¾**:16½in), ending with RS facing.

Armhole shaping

Keep st st correct throughout.

Cast (bind) off 3 sts at beg of next 2 rows. *78(**86**:92:**100**:106) sts*

Cast (bind) off 2 sts at beg of next 2 rows. *74(**82**:88:**96**:102) sts*

Next row (RS): Ssk, k to last 2 sts, k2tog. *72(**80**:86:**94**:100) sts ***

Now work straight in st st (beg with a **WS** row) until armhole measures approx. 18:**18**:20:**20**:22cm (7:**7**:8:**8**:8¾in) from beg of armhole shaping, ending with RS facing.

Shoulder shaping

Cast (bind) off 7(**9**:10:**10**:11) sts at beg of next 4 rows. *44(**44**:46:**54**:56) sts*

Cast (bind) off 9(**9**:10:**12**:13) sts at beg of next 2 rows. *26(**26**:26:**30**:30) sts*

Leave rem 26(**26**:26:**30**:30) sts on a holder at back neck.

FRONT

Work as for Back to **.

Now work straight in st st (beg with a **WS** row) until armhole measures approx. 12:**12**:14:**14**:16cm (4¾:**4¾**:5½:**5½**:6¼in) from beg of armhole shaping, ending with RS facing.

Front neck shaping

With RS facing and keeping st st correct throughout, work over next 30(**34**:37:**39**:42) sts, turn work, leaving all rem sts on a st holder.

Left front neck

Next row (WS): Cast (bind) off 4 sts, p to end. *26(**30**:33:**35**:38) sts*

Work RS row.

Next row (WS): Cast (bind) off 2 sts, p to end. *24(**28**:31:**33**:36) sts*

Work RS row.

Next row (WS): P2tog, p to end. *23(**27**:30:**32**:35) sts*

Now work straight in st st until armhole measures approx. 18:**18**:20:**20**:22cm (7:**7**:8:**8**:8¾in) from beg of armhole shaping, ending with RS facing.

Left shoulder shaping

Next row (RS): Cast (bind) off 7(**9**:10:**10**:11) sts, k to end. *16(**18**:20:**22**:24) sts*

Work **WS** row.

Next row (RS): Cast (bind) off 7(**9**:10:**10**:11) sts, k to end. *9(**9**:10:**12**:13) sts*

Work **WS** row.

Cast (bind) off rem 9(**9**:10:**12**:13) sts.

Centre and right front neck

With RS facing, keep centre 12(**12**:12:**16**:16) sts at front neck on a holder and work on rem 30(**34**:37:**39**:42) sts as folls:

Next row (RS): Cast (bind) off 4 sts, k to end. *26(**30**:33:**35**:38) sts*

Work **WS** row.

Next row (RS): Cast (bind) off 2 sts, k to end.

*24(**28**:31:**33**:36) sts*
Work **WS** row.
Next row (RS): K2tog, k to end. *23(**27**:30:**32**:35) sts*
Now work straight in st st until armhole measures approx. 18:**18**:20:20:22cm (7:**7**:8:**8**:8¾in) from beg of armhole shaping, ending with **WS** facing.

Right shoulder shaping
Next row (WS): Cast (bind) off 7(**9**:10:**10**:11) sts, p to end. *16(**18**:20:**22**:24) sts*
Work RS row.
Next row (WS): Cast (bind) off 7(**9**:10:**10**:11) sts, p to end. *9(**9**:10:**12**:13) sts*
Work RS row.
Cast (bind) off rem 9(**9**:10:**12**:13) sts.

SLEEVES (make 2)
Using 7mm (US size 10½) needles and thumb method, cast on 30(**30**:34:**34**:36) sts.
Row 1 (WS): P.
Row 2: K.
Work Row 1 once more, ending with RS facing.
Now work in rib as folls:
Rib row 1 (RS): *K1, p1; rep from * to end.
Rib Row 1 ONLY rep forms rib.
Cont in rib until work measures 5cm (2in) from cast-on edge, ending with RS facing.
Now work in st st as folls:
Row 1 (RS): K.
Row 2: P.
These 2 rows rep form st st.
Cont in st st WHILST AT THE SAME TIME inc 1 st at each end of next and then every sixth row to 44(**44**:48:**48**:50) sts, ending with RS facing.
Cont straight in st st until work measures approx. 38:**38**:40:42:44cm (15:**15**:15¾:**16½**:17¼in), ending with RS facing.

Armhole shaping
Keep st st correct throughout.
Cast (bind) off 3 sts at beg of next 2 rows.
*38(**38**:42:**42**:44) sts*
Cast (bind) off 2 sts at beg of next 2 rows.
*34(**34**:38:**38**:40) sts*
Next row (RS): Ssk, k to last 2 sts, k2tog.
*32(**32**:36:**36**:38) sts*
Work **WS** row.
Rep last 2 rows four times more. *24(**24**:28:**28**:30) sts*
Next row (RS): Ssk, k to last 2 sts, k2tog.
*22(**22**:26:**26**:28) sts*
Rep last row three times more ending with RS facing. *16(**16**:20:**20**:22) sts*
Cast (bind) off 4 sts at beg of next 2 rows.
*8(**8**:12:**12**:14) sts*
Cast (bind) off.

TIES (make 2)
Using 7mm (US size 10½) needles and thumb method, cast on 26 sts.
Next row (WS): P.
Next row (RS): K.
Next row (WS): P.
Now work in st st with garter st edges as folls:
Row 1 (RS): K.
Row 2: K3, p to last 2 sts, k3.
These 2 rows rep form st st with garter st edges.
Cont straight as set until tie measures 60cm (23½in) from cast-on edge, ending with RS facing.
Work 3 rows of k, ending with WS facing.
Cast (bind) off knitwise.

FINISHING

Press/block all garment pieces.

Join left shoulder seam.

Neckband

Using 7mm (US size 10½) needles, re-join yarn and knit 26(**26**:26:**30**:30) sts left on a holder at back neck, pick up and k 11 sts down left front neck, re-join yarn and k 12 sts left on a holder at front neck, and then pick up and k 11 sts up right front neck. *60(**60**:60:**64**:64) sts*

Next row (WS): *K1, p1; rep from * to end.

Now work in rib as folls:

Rib row 1: *K1, p1; rep from * to end.

Rib Row 1 ONLY rep forms rib.

Work 4 more rows of rib.

Cast (bind) off in rib.

Join right shoulder and neckband seam.

Join centre of sleeve head cast (bind) off to shoulder seam and ease sleeve into armhole of garment body; rep for second sleeve. Join sleeve seams and sew cast-on edge of each tie into side seams (placing top of tie approx. 12cm (4¾in) down from each armhole).

Press/block again if needed.

ISLA

[SET-IN | Contrast Fairisle Sweater]

You can create some amazing combinations when you pair together two different fairisle patterns using the same colour palette. This sweater combines a subtle patterned front with a heavily patterned and traditional striped back. You could wear this garment back to front on those days that you want a brighter look.

TECHNIQUE
Contrast fairisle

SIZE Note sizes are approximate.

	Small	Medium	Large	X Large	XX Large	
To fit	81–86	91–96	101–106	112–117	122–127	cm
	32–34	36–38	40–42	44–46	48–50	in
Actual	140	154	164	176	186	cm
(approx.)	55	60½	64½	69¼	73	in
Length	54	54	58	60	64	cm
(approx.)	21¼	21¼	23	23½	25¼	in
Sleeve seam	38	38	40	42	44	cm
(approx.)	15	15	15¾	16½	17¼	in

YARN
DK (light worsted)
Sample made in
Rowan Alpaca Soft DK
(70% Virgin Wool, 30% Alpaca, approx. 125m/137yd per 50g/1¾oz ball)
7(**8**:8:**9**:10) balls of Trench Coat (**A**)
3(**4**:4:**5**:5) balls of Naples Blue (**B**)
2(**2**:2:**3**:3) balls of Autumn Gold (**C**)
1(**1**:1:**2**:2) balls of Green Teal (**D**)
1(**1**:1:**2**:2) balls of Autumn Purple (**E**)

NEEDLES AND OTHER ITEMS
4mm (US size 6) knitting needles
3 stitch holders

TENSION (GAUGE)
22 sts x 30 rows = 10cm (4in) square working st st on 4mm (US size 6) needles.
22 sts x 25 rows = 10cm (4in) square working front Fairisle (Chart A) on 4mm (US size 6) needles.
22 sts x 26 rows = 10cm (4in) square working back Fairisle (Chart B) on 4mm (US size 6) needles.

ABBREVIATIONS
See page 20

PATTERN NOTE
When working from fairisle charts, read all odd number (RS) rows from right to left and all even number (WS) rows from left to right.

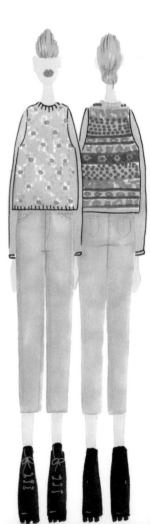

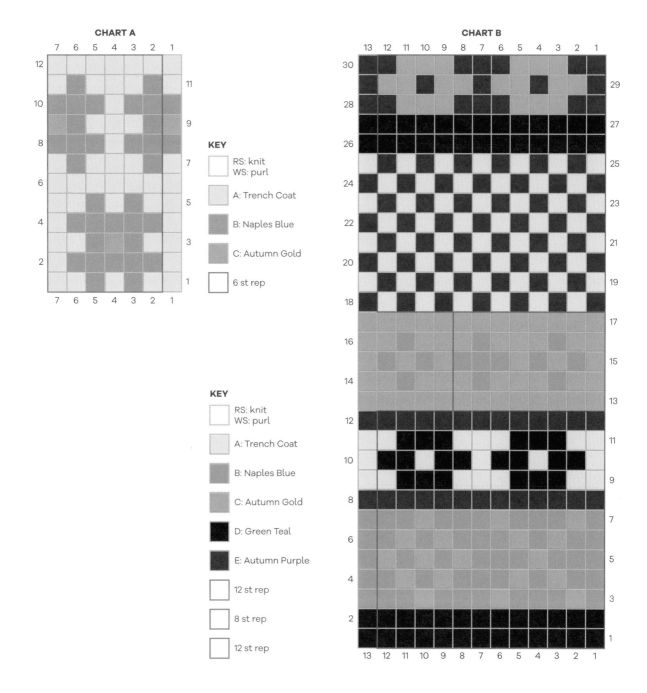

CHART A

CHART B

KEY
- RS: knit / WS: purl
- A: Trench Coat
- B: Naples Blue
- C: Autumn Gold
- 6 st rep

KEY
- RS: knit / WS: purl
- A: Trench Coat
- B: Naples Blue
- C: Autumn Gold
- D: Green Teal
- E: Autumn Purple
- 12 st rep
- 8 st rep
- 12 st rep

MAKE

FRONT

Using 4mm (US size 6) needles and A, cast on 158(**170**:182:**194**:206) sts.

Now work in rib as folls:

Row 1 (RS): *K2, p2; rep from * to last 2 sts, k2.

Row 2: P2, *k2, P2; rep from * to end.

These 2 rows rep form rib.

Cont in rib until work measures approx. 3cm (1¼in) from cast-on edge, ending with **WS** facing.

Next row (WS): P2, *k2, p2; rep from * to last 4 sts, k2, p2tog. *157(**169**:181:**193**:205) sts* **

Now work in st st as folls:

Next row (RS): K.

Next row: P.

Now place Chart A as folls:

Row 1 (RS): K1 A, *[k1 A, k1 B] twice, k2 A; rep from * to end.

Row 2: *P1 A, p5 B; rep from * to last st, p1 A.

Row 3: K1 A, *k1 A, k1 B, k1 C, k1 B, k2 A; rep from * to end.

Row 4: *P1 A, p5 B; rep from * to last st, p1 A.

Row 5: K1 A, *[k1 A, k1 B] twice, k2 A; rep from * to end.

Row 6: P in A.

Row 7: K1 A, *k1 B, k3 A, k1 B, k1 A; rep from * to end.

Row 8: *P3 B, p1 A, p2 B; rep from * to last st, p1 B.

Row 9: K1 C, *k1 B, k3 A, k1 B, k1 C; rep from * to end.

Row 10: *P3 B, p1 A, p2 B; rep from * to last st, p1 B.

Row 11: K1 A, *k1 B, k3 A, k1 B, k1 A; rep from * to end.

Row 12: P in A.

These 12 rows rep form fairisle patt from Chart A.

Cont in fairisle patt until work measures approx. 36:**36**:38:**40**:42cm (14:**14**:15:**15¾**:16½in) from cast-on edge, ending with RS facing.

Armhole shaping

***Keep fairisle patt correct throughout.

Cast (bind) off 4 sts at beg of next 4 rows.

*141(**153**:165:**177**:189) sts*

Cast (bind) off 2 sts at beg of next 2 rows.

*137(**149**:161:**173**:185) sts*

Now work straight keeping fairisle patt correct until armhole measures approx. 14:**14**:16:**16**:18cm (5½:**5½**:6¼:**6¼**:7in) from beg of armhole shaping, ending with RS facing.****

Front neck shaping

Work in fairisle patt over next 59(**65**:71:**77**:83) sts, then turn work leaving centre 19 sts on one holder at centre front neck and rem 59(**65**:71:**77**:83) sts on a second holder.

Now work neck shaping whilst keeping fairisle patt correct as folls:

Next row (WS): Cast (bind) off 7 sts, patt to end. *52(**58**:64:**70**:76) sts*

Work RS row in patt.

Next row (WS): Cast (bind) off 4 sts, patt to end. *48(**54**:60:**66**:72) sts*

Work RS row in patt.

Next row (WS): Cast (bind) off 2 sts, patt to end. *46(**52**:58:**64**:70) sts*

Work RS row in patt.

Next row (WS): P2tog, patt to end. *45(**51**:57:**63**:69) sts*

Now work straight keeping fairisle patt correct until armhole measures approx. 18:**18**:20:**20**:22cm (7:**7**:8:**8**:8¾in) from beg of armhole shaping, ending with RS facing.

Left shoulder shaping

Cast (bind) off 15(**17**:19:**21**:23) sts at beg on next 2 RS rows. *15(**17**:19:**21**:23) sts*

Work **WS** row in patt.

Cast (bind) off rem 15(**17**:19:**21**:23) sts.

With RS facing, re-join yarn to 59(**65**:71:**77**:83) sts and work second side of front neck whilst keeping fairisle patt correct as folls:

Next row (RS): Cast (bind) off 7 sts, patt to end. *52(**58**:64:**70**:76) sts*
Work **WS** row in patt.
Next row (RS): Cast (bind) off 4 sts, patt to end. *48(**54**:60:**66**:72) sts*
Work **WS** row in patt.
Next row (RS): Cast (bind) off 2 sts, patt to end. *46(**52**:58:**64**:70) sts*
Work **WS** row in patt.
Next row (RS): K2tog, patt to end.
*45(**51**:57:**63**:69) sts*
Now work straight keeping fairisle patt correct until armhole measures approx. 18:**18**:20:**20**:22cm (7:**7**:8:**8**:8¾in) from beg of armhole shaping, ending with **WS** facing.

Right shoulder shaping
Cast (bind) off 15(**17**:19:**21**:23) sts at beg on next 2 **WS** rows. *15(**17**:19:**21**:23) sts*
Work RS row in patt.
Cast (bind) off rem 15(**17**:19:**21**:23) sts.

BACK
Work as for Front to **.
Now place Chart B as folls:
Row 1 (RS): K in D.
Row 2: P in D.
Row 3: K1 A, *[k1 C, k3 A] three times; rep from * to end.
Row 4: *P2 B, p1 A, p1 B, p1 A, p3 B, p1 A, p1 B, p1 A, p1 B; rep from * to last st, p1 B.
Cont as set above completing Chart B rows 5–30. These 30 rows set fairisle patt, rep them until work measures approx. 36:**36**:38:**40**:42cm (14:**14**:15:**15¾**:16½in) from cast-on edge, ending with RS facing.

Armhole shaping
Work from *** to **** from front armhole shaping.
Shoulder shaping
Keeping fairisle patt correct, cast (bind) off 15(**17**:19:**21**:23) sts at beg of next 6 rows. *47 sts*
Leave these 47 sts on a third holder for neckband.

SLEEVES (make 2)
Using 4mm (US size 6) needles and A, cast on 48(**48**:52:**52**:58) sts.
Now work in garter st as folls:
Row 1 (RS): K.
Row 2: K.
Work these 2 rows once more.
Now work in st st as folls:
Row 1 (RS): K.
Row 2: P.
These 2 rows rep form st st.
Cont in st st WHILST AT THE SAME TIME inc 1 st at each end of next and then every eighth row to 70(**70**:80:**80**:84) sts, ending with RS facing.
Cont straight in st st until work measures approx. 38:**38**:40:**42**:44cm (15:**15**:15¾:**16½**:17¼in), ending with RS facing.

Armhole shaping
Keep st st correct throughout.
Cast (bind) off 4 sts at beg of next 4 rows.
*54(**54**:64:**64**:68) sts*
Cast (bind) off 2 sts at beg of next 2 rows.
*50(**50**:60:**60**:64) sts*
Sleeve head shaping
Work 4 rows of st st.
Dec 1 st at each end of next row and next alt row.
*46(**46**:56:**56**:60) sts*
Work 3 rows ending with RS facing.
Dec 1 st at each end of next row.
*44(**44**:54:**54**:58) sts*

HINTS AND TIPS

▶ Working with pattern shouldn't be boring and mixing patterns can work really well, as can picking your own exciting colour palette.

◉ When choosing your own colour palette think about placement and proportion. You can use graph paper and colour in the individual squares to help plan your colour palette. Alternatively, you could use Microsoft Excel or Stitch Mastery.

Work last 4 rows once more. *42(**42**:52:**52**:56) sts*
Work **WS** row.
Dec 1 st at each end of next row and next alt row.
*38(**38**:48:**48**:52) sts*
Work **WS** row.
Dec 1 st at each end of next 8 rows.
*22(**22**:32:**32**:36) sts*
Cast (bind) off 3 sts at beg of next 2 rows.
*16(**16**:26:**26**:30) sts*
Cast (bind) off 4(**4**:6:**6**:8) sts at beg of next 2 rows.
*8(**8**:14:**14**:14) sts*
Cast (bind) off rem 8(**8**:14:**14**:14) sts.

FINISHING
Press/block all garment pieces.
Join left shoulder seam.
Neckband
Using 4mm (US size 6) needles and A and with RS
facing, re-join yarn and k to 47 sts left on a holder
at back neck, pick up and k 15 sts down left front
neck, re-join yarn and k 19 sts left on a holder at
front neck and then pick up and k 15 sts up right
front neck. *96 sts*
Next row (WS): K.
Next row (RS): K.
With WS facing, cast (bind) off knitwise.
Join right shoulder and neckband seam.
Join centre of sleeve head cast (bind) off to
shoulder seam and ease sleeve into armhole
of garment body; rep for second sleeve. Join
sleeve and side seams.
Press/block again if needed.

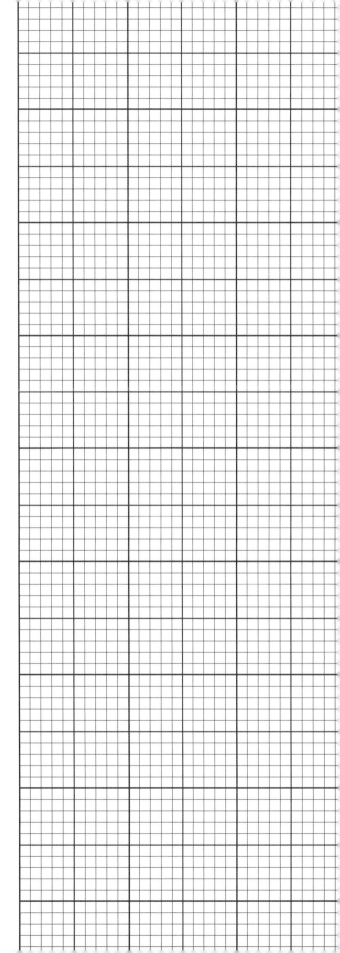

Raglan

This shape is perhaps the most complicated to knit but the most satisfying when achieved. I adore a raglan yoke: I love to knit them, I love to design them and I definitely love wearing them. A raglan-yoke sweater has to be the most worn garment I have in my wardrobe, a true classic staple that is always on trend.

My favourite project from this section is Sunflower on pages 130–135. I could spend hours in a good haberdashery store and find a zip simply satisfying. Mustard is my favourite colour (other than pink of course), and I love the iconic simplicity of a fisherman's rib. You can see exactly why this garment is my dream sweater.

Within this section you will learn how to use zips in knitwear, knit bobbles into the shape of a heart (you're welcome!), and work a fairisle yoke and colour stranding in the round.

EVELYN

[RAGLAN | Bobble Heart Yoke]

SUNFLOWER

[RAGLAN | Zipped Back Sweater]

PAGES 136–141

ROSE

[RAGLAN | Houndstooth Yoke Sweater]

PAGES 142–147

POPPY

[RAGLAN | Faux Tartan Sweater]

DAISY

[RAGLAN | Fairisle Yoke Sweater]

EVELYN

[RAGLAN | Bobble Heart Yoke]

Bobbles are one of the most rewarding and fun stitch patterns and you can't beat them when they are formed into a lovely heart shape. This is a chic chunky sweater that will go with everything in your wardrobe.

TECHNIQUE
Bobbles in the round

SIZE Note sizes are approximate.

	Small	Medium	Large	X Large	XX Large	
To fit	81–86	91–96	101–106	112–117	122–127	cm
	32–34	36–38	40–42	44–46	48–50	in
Actual	128	138	146	156	164	cm
(approx.)	50½	54¼	57½	61½	64½	in
Length	56	60	62	64	65	cm
(approx.)	22	23½	24½	25¼	25½	in
Sleeve seam	43	45.5	47	47	49	cm
(approx.)	17	18	18½	18½	19¼	in

YARN
Chunky (bulky)
Sample made in
Rowan Big Wool
(100% Wool, approx. 80m/87yd
per 100g/3½oz ball)
8(**9**:10:**11**:11) balls of Biscotti

NEEDLES AND OTHER ITEMS
10mm (US size 15) straight needles
10mm (US size 15) long circular needle
9mm (US size 13) straight needles
3 large stitch holders
4 stitch markers

TENSION (GAUGE)
9 sts x 12.5 rows = 10cm (4in) square
working reverse st st on 10mm
(US size 15) needles.

ABBREVIATIONS
See page 20

SPECIAL ABBREVIATIONS
MB (make bobble): k into front, back
and front again of next st, turn, p3, turn,
k3, turn, p3, turn, slip 1 st, k2tog, psso
(bobble complete)

MAKE

FRONT AND BACK (make both the same)
Using 10mm (US size 15) straight needles and thumb method, cast on 58(**62**:66:**70**:74) sts.
Row 1 (RS): *K2, p2; rep from * to last 2 sts, k2.
Row 2: *P2, k2; rep from * to last 2 sts, p2.
These 2 rows form rib, rep them twice more.
Now work in rev st st as folls:
Row 1 (RS): P.
Row 2: K.
Rep these 2 rows until work measures approx. 32:**32**:34:**34**:34cm (12½:**12½**:13½:**13½**:13½in), ending with RS facing.
Knitter's note: Work fewer or more rows here for a shorter or longer garment.
Working in rev st st, cast (bind) off 4 sts at beg of next 2 rows. *50(**54**:58:**62**:66) sts*
Leave rem sts on a holder.

SLEEVES (make 2)
Using 10mm (US size 15) straight needles and thumb method, cast on 18(**18**:22:**22**:26) sts.
Row 1 (RS): *K2, p2; rep from * to last 2 sts, k2.
Row 2: *P2, k2; rep from * to last 2 sts, p2.
These 2 rows form rib, rep them twice more.
Now work in rev st st as folls:
Row 1 (RS): P.
Row 2: K.
These 2 rows form rev st st.
Cont in rev st st WHILST AT THE SAME TIME inc 1 st at each end of next and then every fourth row to 36(**36**:40:**40**:44) sts, ending with RS facing.
Cont straight in rev st st until work measures 43:**45.5**:47:**47**:49cm (17:**18**:18½:**18½**:19¼in), ending with RS facing.
Working in rev st st, cast (bind) off 4 sts at beg of next 2 rows. *28(**28**:32:**32**:36) sts*
Leave rem sts on a holder.

YOKE
Keeping rev st st in the round correct (P every round) throughout, join all garment pieces to form yoke as folls:
Using 10mm (US size 15) circular needle and with RS facing, re-join yarn and work across 28(**28**:32:**32**:36) sts for first sleeve, PM, work across 50(**54**:58:**62**:66) sts for front, PM, work across 28(**28**:32:**32**:36) sts for second sleeve, PM, and then work across 50(**54**:58:**62**:66) sts for back. *156(**164**:180:**188**:204) sts*
Beg working in rounds.
Next round: P, slipping markers.
Now work yoke dec as folls:
Yoke round 1: P1, p2tog, p22(**22**:26:**26**:30), p2tog, p1, SM, p1, p2tog, p44(**48**:52:**56**:60), p2tog, p1, SM, p1, p2tog, p22(**22**:26:**26**:30), p2tog, p1, SM, p1, p2tog, p44(**48**:52:**56**:60), p2tog, p1. *148(**156**:172:**180**:196) sts*
Yoke round 2: P, slipping markers.
Rep these 2 rounds 2(**3**:4:**4**:6) times more. *132(**132**:140:**148**:148) sts*
Third size only
Next round: [K15, k2tog] 8 times, k4. *132 sts*
Fourth and fifth sizes only
Next round: [K7, k2tog] 16 times, k4. *132 sts*
All sizes
*132(**132**:132:**132**:132) sts*
Now work bobble hearts (keeping st markers in place throughout) as folls:
Round 1: *P5, MB, p5; rep from * to end.
Round 2: P.
Round 3: *P3, MB, p3, MB, p3; rep from * to end.
Round 4: P.
Round 5: *P1, MB, p7, MB, p1; rep from * to end.
Round 6: P.
Round 7: *P1, MB, p3, MB, p3, MB, p1; rep from * to end.

Round 8: P to last st, PM to denote beg/end.
Round 9 (dec): Sl first st (st from last round), k2tog, psso, *p1, MB, p3, MB, p2, **sk2po; rep from * ending last rep at **. *108 sts*
Round 10: P.
Rep Yoke Rounds 1 and 2 again as set a further 4 times. *76 sts*
Note: remove st markers when working next round.
Next round (dec): P11, [p2tog, p1] 9 times, p12, [p2tog, p1] 9 times, p1. *58 sts*
Next round (dec): K2tog, k27, k2tog, k27. *56 sts*
Change to 9mm (US size 13) needles.
Now work in rib as folls:
Rib row 1 (WS): *K2, p2; rep from * to last 2 sts, k2.
Rib row 2: *P2, k2; rep from * to last 2 sts, p2.
These 2 rows form rib.
Cont until rib measures approx. 2.5cm (1in) ending with Rib Row 1.
Cast (bind) off in rib with RS facing.

FINISHING

Press/block all garment pieces.
Join side, underarm and sleeve seams using mattress stitch or preferred method.
Fasten off any loose ends.
Press/block again if needed.

HINTS AND TIPS

▶ If you have a bobble technique you prefer you can use it instead of the MB in the pattern – or if you prefer a bigger bobble, knit into the front, back, front, back and front again working over 5 sts instead of the 3 stated in the pattern.

○ Take time when working the bobbles and once completed make sure each bobble is poking out of the front of the fabric and not through the back.

SUNFLOWER

[RAGLAN | Zipped Back Sweater]

This is my favourite of all the projects in this book – so much so that you can find me wearing it in my author's photo on page 159. I love the mustard and the zip detailing, while the stitch used is super therapeutic and finishes the zip off nicely.

TECHNIQUE
Zip in knitwear – garment can be worn back to front

SIZE Note sizes are approximate.

	Small	Medium	Large	X Large	XX Large	
To fit	81–86	91–96	101–106	112–117	122–127	cm
	32–34	36–38	40–42	44–46	48–50	in
Actual	120	130	140	150	160	cm
(approx.)	47¼	51¼	55	59	63	in
Length	45	48	50	52	56	cm
(approx.)	17¾	19	19¾	20½	22	in
Sleeve seam	43	45.5	47	47	49	cm
(approx.)	17	18	18½	18½	19¼	in

YARN
DK (light worsted)
Sample made in
Lang Yarns Cashmere Cotton
(55% Cashmere, 45% Cotton, approx.
85m/93yd per 25g/⅞oz ball)
18(**19**:20:**21**:22) balls of Field

NEEDLES AND OTHER ITEMS
4mm (US size 6) straight needles
4mm (US size 6) long circular needle
3 large stitch holders
4 stitch markers
Approx. 60cm (24in) long black
tape continuous zip
Scissors
Pins

TENSION (GAUGE)
23 sts x 47 rows = 10cm (4in) square
working fisherman's rib on 4mm
(US size 6) needles.

ABBREVIATIONS
See page 20

MAKE

FRONT

Using 4mm (US size 6) straight needles and thumb method, cast on 138(**150**:162:**172**:184) sts.

Row 1 (WS): P.

Row 2: *P1, k next st in row below allowing old st to drop off needle; rep from * to last 2 sts, p2. Row 2 ONLY rep forms fisherman's rib.

Cont in fisherman's rib until work measures approx. 32:**34**:34:**36**:38cm (12½:**13½**:13½:**14**:15in), ending with RS facing.

Knitter's note: Work fewer or more rows here for a shorter or longer garment.

Working in fisherman's rib, cast (bind) off 8 sts at beg of next 2 rows. *122(**134**:146:**156**:168) sts*

Leave rem sts on a holder.

RIGHT BACK

Using 4mm (US size 6) straight needles and thumb method, cast on 70(**76**:82:**86**:92) sts.

Row 1 (WS): P.

Row 2: *P1, k next st in row below allowing old st to drop off needle; rep from * to last 2 sts, p2. Row 2 ONLY rep forms fisherman's rib.

Cont in fisherman's rib until work measures approx. 32:**34**:34:**36**:38cm (12½:**13½**:13½:**14**:15in), ending with RS facing.

Knitter's note: Work fewer or more rows here for a shorter or longer garment.

Cast (bind) off 8 sts, work in fisherman's rib to end. *62(**68**:74:**78**:84) sts*

Keeping fisherman's rib correct, work 1 row, ending with RS facing.

Leave rem sts on a holder.

LEFT BACK

Using 4mm (US size 6) straight needles and thumb method, cast on 70(**76**:82:**86**:92) sts.

Row 1 (WS): P.

Row 2: *P1, k next st in row below allowing old st to drop off needle; rep from * to last 2 sts, p2. Row 2 ONLY rep forms fisherman's rib.

Cont in fisherman's rib until work measures approx. 32:**34**:34:**36**:38cm (12½:**13½**:13½:**14**:15in), ending with **WS** facing.

Knitter's note: Work fewer or more rows here for a shorter or longer garment.

Cast (bind) off 8 sts, work in fisherman's rib to end. *62(**68**:74:**78**:84) sts*

Leave rem sts on a holder.

SLEEVES (make 2)

Using 4mm (US size 6) straight needles and thumb method, cast on 42(**42**:48:**48**:52) sts.

Row 1 (WS): P.

Row 2: *P1, k next st in row below allowing old st to drop off needle; rep from * to last 2 sts, p2. Row 2 ONLY rep forms fisherman's rib.

Cont in fisherman's rib WHILST AT THE SAME TIME inc 1 st at each end of next and then every tenth row to 74(**74**:78:**82**:88) sts, ending with RS facing.

Cont straight in fisherman's rib until work measures 43:**45.5**:47:**47**:49cm (17:**18**:18½:**18½**:19¼in), ending with RS facing.

Working in fisherman's rib, cast (bind) off 8 sts at beg of next 2 rows. *58(**58**:62:**66**:72) sts*

Leave rem sts on a holder.

YOKE

Keeping fisherman's rib correct throughout, join all garment pieces to form yoke as folls:

Using 4mm (US size 6) circular needle and with RS facing, re-join yarn and work across 62(**68**:74:**78**:84) sts for left back, PM, work across

58(**58**:62:**66**:72) sts for first sleeve, PM, work across 122(**134**:146:**156**:168) sts for back, PM, work across 58(**58**:62:**66**:72) sts for second sleeve, PM and then work across 62(**68**:74:**78**:84) sts for right back. *362(**386**:418:**444**:480) sts*

Next row (WS): Work in fisherman's rib to 3 sts before first marker, p3, *SM, p3, work in fisherman's rib to 3 sts before next marker, p3; rep from * three times, SM, p3, work in fisherman's rib to end. Now work yoke dec as folls:

Yoke row 1: Work in fisherman's rib over next 59(**65**:71:**75**:81) sts, k2tog, k1, SM, k1, ssk, work in fisherman's rib over next 52(**52**:56:**60**:66) sts, k2tog, k1, SM, k1, ssk, work in fisherman's rib over next 116(**128**:140:**150**:162) sts, k2tog, k1, SM, k1, ssk, work in fisherman's rib over next 52(**52**:56:**60**:66) sts, k2tog, k1, SM, k1, ssk, work in fisherman's rib to end. *354(**378**:410:**436**:472) sts*

Yoke row 2: Work in fisherman's rib to 3 sts before first marker, p3, *SM, p3, work in fisherman's rib to 3 sts before next marker, p3; rep from * three times, SM, p3, work in fisherman's rib to end. These 2 rounds form yoke dec, rep them 26(**26**:30:**32**:34) times more. *146(**170**:170:**180**:200) sts*

Knitter's note: Remove markers when completing next row on all sizes.

First size only
Next row (RS): [K4, k2tog] 24 times, k2. *122 sts*

Second and third sizes only
Next row (RS): K2, [k1, k2tog] 12 times, k11, [k1, k2tog] 24 times, k10, [k1, k2tog] 12 times, k3. *122 sts*

Fourth size only
Next row (RS): K6, *[k1, k2tog] 27 times, k6; rep from * once more. *126 sts*

Fifth size only
Next row (RS): *[K13, k2tog] 37 times, k13; rep from * once more. *126 sts*

All sizes
*122(**122**:122:**126**:126) sts*
Now work in rib as folls:
Rib row 1 (WS): *K2, p2; rep from * to last 2 sts, k2.
Rib row 2: *P2, k2; rep from * to last 2 sts, p2.
These 2 rows rep form rib.
Cont in rib for approx. 2.5cm (1in), ending with Rib Row 1.
Cast (bind) off in rib with RS facing.

FINISHING
Press/block all garment pieces.
Join side, underarm and sleeve seams using mattress stitch or preferred method.
Fasten off any loose ends.
Press/block again if needed.
Add the zip
Cut the zip to the length of the garment (see Hints and Tips), or your desired length.
Pin the zip in place with RS facing to the WS of the garment fabric.

Thread a large-eyed pointed needle with a long length of yarn, and sew the zip in place as folls: bring the threaded needle up through the zip tape and out between the garment fabric and the zip. Now insert the needle back through the same point you just came up through, going through both the zip tape and the garment fabric and creating a loop of thread (see photograph), then bring the needle back up through the zip tape and garment fabric approx. 0.5cm (¼in) away and going up through the loop of thread. Pull tight but do not pucker the garment fabric. Continue this method of sewing until the zip is fully sewn in. Fasten off securely.

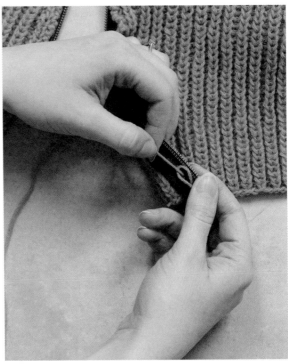

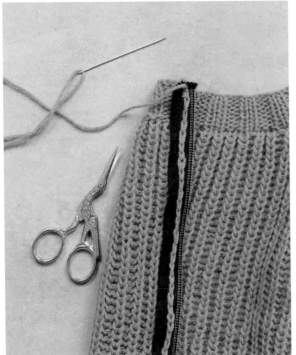

HINTS AND TIPS

▶ Cut the zip to the length of the garment plus approx. 4cm (1⅝in), which allows a bit extra at each end. This can be folded back and secured at the back of the work, creating a neater edge for the zip.

● The technique given for sewing in the zip creates a stable but flexible stitch so that the zip isn't sewn in too tightly, which would pucker the fabric.

ROSE

[RAGLAN | Houndstooth Yoke Sweater]

Houndstooth is such a classic print and although I love its original black and white colour scheme, don't these bright colours really bring this print to life!

TECHNIQUE
Colour work – stranding in the round

SIZE Note sizes are approximate.

	Small	Medium	Large	X Large	XX Large	
To fit	81–86	91–96	101–106	112–117	122–127	cm
	32–34	36–38	40–42	44–46	48–50	in
Actual	110	120	130	141	151	cm
(approx.)	43¼	47¼	51¼	55½	59½	in
Length	53	54	58	60	62	cm
(approx.)	21	21¼	23	23½	24½	in
Sleeve seam	43	45.5	47	47	49	cm
(approx.)	17	18	18½	18½	19¼	in

YARN
Aran (worsted)
Sample made in
West Yorkshire Spinners Bluefaced
Leicester Aran
(100% Bluefaced Leicester, approx.
83m/91yd per 50g/1¾oz ball)
9(**10**:11:**12**:13) balls of Teal (**A**)
2(**2**:3:**3**:3) balls of Coral (**B**)

NEEDLES AND OTHER ITEMS
5mm (US size 8) straight needles
5mm (US size 8) long circular needle
3 large stitch holders
4 stitch markers

TENSION (GAUGE)
18 sts x 24 rows = 10cm (4in) square
working st st on 5mm (US size 8) needles.
22.5 sts x 23 rows = 10cm (4in) square
working houndstooth fairisle on
5mm (US size 8) needles.

ABBREVIATIONS
See page 20

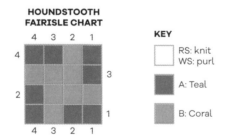

**HOUNDSTOOTH
FAIRISLE CHART**

KEY

RS: knit
WS: purl

A: Teal

B: Coral

MAKE

BACK
Using 5mm (US size 8) straight needles and A, cast on 102(**110**:118:**126**:138) sts.
Row 1 (RS): *K2, p2; rep from * to last 2 sts, k2.
Row 2: *P2, k2; rep from * to last 2 sts, p2.
These 2 rows rep form rib.
Cont in rib until work measures approx. 3.5cm (1½in) from cast-on edge, ending with **WS** facing.
Next row (WS): P.
Now work in st st as folls:
Row 1 (RS): K.
Row 2: P.
These 2 rows rep form st st.
Cont in st st until work measures approx. 32:**32**:34:**34**:34cm (12½:**12½**:13½:**13½**:13½in), ending with RS facing.
Working in st st, cast (bind) off 8 sts at beg of next 2 rows. *86(**94**:102:**110**:122) sts*
Leave rem sts on a holder.

FRONT
Using 5mm (US size 8) straight needles and A, cast on 102(**110**:118:**126**:138) sts.
Row 1 (RS): *K2, p2; rep from * to last 2 sts, k2.
Row 2: *P2, k2; rep from * to last 2 sts, p2.
These 2 rows rep form rib.
Cont in rib until work measures approx. 3.5cm (1½in) from cast-on edge, ending with **WS** facing.
Next row (inc, WS): P7(**5**:16:**14**:2), [M1p, p4:**4**:3:**3**:4] 22(**26**:30:**34**:34) times, p7(**1**:12:**10**:0).
*124(**136**:148:**160**:172) sts*
Now work houndstooth fairisle (using chart if needed) as folls:
Row 1 (RS): *K2 A, k1 B, k1 A; rep from * to end.
Row 2: *P1 A, p3 B; rep from * to end.
Row 3: *K1 A, k3 B; rep from * to end.
Row 4: *P2 A, p1 B, p1 A; rep from * to end.

These 4 rows rep form houndstooth fairisle.
Cont in houndstooth fairisle until work measures approx. 32:**32**:34:**34**:34cm (12½:**12½**:13½:**13½**:13½in), ending with RS facing.
Working in houndstooth fairisle, cast (bind) off 8 sts at beg of next 2 rows. *108(**120**:132:**144**:156) sts*
Leave rem sts on a holder.

SLEEVES (make 2)
Using 5mm (US size 8) straight needles and A, cast on 34(**34**:38:**38**:42) sts.
Row 1 (RS): *K2, p2; rep from * to last 2 sts, k2.
Row 2: *P2, k2; rep from * to last 2 sts, p2.
These 2 rows rep form rib.
Cont in rib until work measures approx. 3.5cm (1½in) from cast-on edge ending with **WS** facing.
Next row (WS): P.
Now work in st st as folls:
Row 1: K.
Row 2: P.
These 2 rows rep form st st.
Cont in st st WHILST AT THE SAME TIME inc 1 st at each end of next and then every eighth row to 58(**58**:62:**64**:68) sts, ending with RS facing.
Cont straight in st st until work measures 43:**45.5**:47:**47**:49cm (17:**18**:18½:**18½**:19¼in), ending with RS facing.
Working in st st, cast (bind) off 8 sts at beg of next 2 rows. *42(**42**:46:**48**:52) sts*
Leave rem sts on a holder.

YOKE
Keep st st over back and sleeves and houndstooth fairisle over front correct throughout (if following chart for houndstooth read each row from right to left), join all garment pieces to form yoke as folls:
PM to indicate beg/end of each round (slip at beg of each round).

HINTS AND TIPS

▶ Working a plain knit round/row before beginning the neckband rib stops the colour work from below leaking into the rib when you work a purl stitch. You will still get the same result if working this round as an extra decrease round.

◉ When stranding the yarn at the back of the work for fairisle, I like to strand each shade of yarn in a particular order – for example, I always strand the main shade (A) over the top and any further shades below. This helps to create a neater and flatter fabric.

Using 5mm (US size 8) circular needle, re-join yarn and k across 42(**42**:46:**48**:52) sts for first sleeve using A, PM, work in houndstooth fairisle across 108(**120**:132:**144**:156) sts for front, PM, k across 42(**42**:46:**48**:52) sts for second sleeve using A, PM, and then k across 86(**94**:102:**110**:122) sts for back using A. *278(**298**:326:**350**:382) sts*
Beg working in rounds.

Next round: K to first marker using A, SM, work in houndstooth fairisle to second marker, SM, k to third marker using A, SM, k to end using A.
Now work first set of yoke dec as folls:

Yoke round 1: K42(**42**:46:**48**:52), SM, k1, ssk, work houndstooth fairisle over next 102(**114**:126:**138**:150) sts, k2tog, k1, SM, k42(**42**:46:**48**:52), SM, k1, ssk, k80(**88**:96:**104**:116) sts, k2tog, k1. *274(**294**:322:**346**:378) sts*

Yoke round 2: K to first marker, SM, work in houndstooth fairisle to second marker, SM, k to third marker, SM, k to end.
These 2 rounds rep form first set of yoke dec, rep them 7(**8**:9:**10**:11) times more. *246(**262**:286:**306**:334) sts*
Now work second set of yoke dec as folls:

Yoke round 1: K1, ssk, k36(**36**:40:**42**:46), k2tog, k1, SM, k1, ssk, work houndstooth fairisle over next 86(**96**:106:**116**:126) sts, k2tog, k1, SM, k1, ssk, k36(**36**:40:**42**:46), k2tog, k1, SM, k1, ssk, k64(**70**:76:**82**:92), k2tog, k1. *238(**254**:278:**298**:326) sts*

Yoke round 2: K to first marker, SM, work in houndstooth fairisle to second marker, SM, k to third marker, SM, k to end.
These 2 rounds rep form second set of yoke dec, rep them 13(**14**:15:**16**:18) times more. *134(**142**:158:**170**:182) sts*

Next round (dec): K14(**12**:14:**14**:14), [k2tog] 32(**36**:40:**44**:47) times, k14(**12**:14:**14**:14), [k2(**5**:1:**1**:1), k2tog] 10(**6**:14:**14**:19) times, k2(**4**:8:**12**:3). *92(**98**:104:**112**:116) sts*
Change to A.

Knitter's note: If neck is wider than you would prefer, replace the next knit round with a further decrease round; you could work another Yoke Round 1 from the second set of yoke decreases and decrease a further 8 sts.

Next round: K.
Now work in rib as folls:

Rib round: *K2, p2; rep from * to end.
This round rep forms rib.
Cont in rib for approx. 3.5cm (1½in).
Cast (bind) off in rib.

FINISHING

Press/block all garment pieces.
Join side, underarm and sleeve seams using mattress stitch or preferred method.
Fasten off any loose ends.
Press/block again if needed.

POPPY

[RAGLAN | Faux Tartan Sweater]

Tartan is an iconic pattern and can sometimes be hard to achieve – it's usually worked with intarsia. I've designed this project to allow you to achieve the amazing tartan look without all the hard work. It will also help bring out your creative side when deciding the darning placement.

TECHNIQUE
Stripes and darning – weaving in method

SIZE Note sizes are approximate.

	Small	Medium	Large	X Large	XX Large	
To fit	81–86	91–96	101–106	112–117	122–127	cm
	32–34	36–38	40–42	44–46	48–50	in
Actual	120	130	140	150	160	cm
(approx.)	47¼	51¼	55	59	63	in
Length (back)	61	63	64	67	71	cm
(approx.)	24	24¾	25¼	26½	28	in
Sleeve seam	24	24	26	28	30	cm
(approx.)	9½	9½	10¼	11	11¾	in

YARN
4ply (sport)
Sample made in
Debbie Bliss Fine Donegal
(95% Wool, 5% Cashmere, approx.
380m/416yd per 100g/3½oz ball)
4(**4**:5:**6**:7) balls of Deep Rose (**A**)
1(**2**:2:**2**:2) balls of Teal (**B**)

NEEDLES AND OTHER ITEMS
3.25mm (US size 3) straight needles
3.25mm (US size 3) long circular needle
3 large stitch holders
4 stitch markers

TENSION (GAUGE)
26 sts x 50 rows = 10cm (4in) square
working garter st on 3.25mm (US size 3)
needles.

ABBREVIATIONS
See page 20

MAKE

BACK

Using 3.25mm (US size 3) straight needles and A, cast on 156(**170**:182:**196**:208) sts.

Now work in garter st as folls:

Row 1: K.

Row 2: K.

These 2 rows rep form garter st.

Now work in striped garter st as folls:

Using A, work 14 rows of garter st.

Using B, work 4 rows of garter st.

Using A, work 8 rows of garter st.

Using B, work 2 rows of garter st.

Using A, work 8 rows of garter st.

Using B, work 4 rows of garter st.

Using A, work 14 rows of garter st.

Using B, work 2 rows of garter st.

These 56 rows rep form striped garter st.**

Cont in striped garter st until work measures approx. 44:**46**:46:**48**:50cm (17¼:**18**:18:**19**:19¾in), ending with RS facing.

Working in garter st, cast (bind) off 10 sts at beg of next 2 rows. *136(**150**:162:**176**:188) sts*

Leave rem sts on a holder.

FRONT

Work as for Back to **.

Cont in striped garter st until work measures approx. 32:**34**:34:**36**:38cm (12½:**13½**:13½:**14**:15in), ending with RS facing.

Working in garter st, cast (bind) off 10 sts at beg of next 2 rows. *136(**150**:162:**176**:188) sts*

Leave rem sts on a holder.

SLEEVES (make 2)

Using 3.25mm (US size 3) straight needles and A, cast on 62(**62**:68:**72**:78)sts.

Now work in garter st as folls:

Row 1: K.

Row 2: K.

These 2 rows rep form garter st.

Now work in striped garter st as given for Back WHILST AT THE SAME TIME in 1 st at each end of next and then every tenth row to 84(**84**:88:**94**:98) sts, ending with RS facing.

Cont straight in striped garter st until work measures 24:**24**:26:**28**:30cm (9½:**9½**:10¼:**11**:11¾in), ending with RS facing.

Working in garter st, cast (bind) off 10 sts at beg of next 2 rows. *64(**64**:68:**74**:78) sts*

Leave rem sts on a holder.

YOKE

Now join all garment pieces to form yoke, working in rounds and keeping striped sequence correct throughout. PM to indicate beg/end of round (slip at beg of each round).

Using 3.25mm (US size 3) circular needle, re-join yarn and k across 64(**64**:68:**74**:78) sts for first sleeve, PM, k across 136(**150**:162:**176**:188) sts for front, PM, k across 64(**64**:68:**74**:78) sts for second sleeve, PM and then k across 136(**150**:162:**176**:188) sts for back. *400(**428**:460:**500**:532) sts*

Next round: P.

Now work yoke dec (keeping striped sequence correct as set above) as folls:

Yoke round 1: K1, ssk, k58(**58**:62:**68**:72), k2tog, k1, SM, k1, ssk, k130(**144**:156:**170**:182), k2tog, k1, SM, k1, ssk, k58(**58**:62:**68**:72), k2tog, k1, SM, k1, ssk, k130(**144**:156:**170**:182), k2tog, k1. *392(**420**:452:**492**:524) sts*

Yoke round 2: P to first marker, SM, p to second marker, SM, p to third marker, SM, p to end.

Yoke round 3: K to first marker, SM, k to second marker, SM, k to third marker, SM, k to end.

Yoke round 4: P1, p2tog, p56(**56**:60:**66**:70), p2tog, p1, SM, p1, p2tog, p128(**142**:154:**168**:180), p2tog, p1, SM, p1, p2tog, p56(**56**:60:**66**:70), p2tog, p1, SM, p1, p2tog, p128(**142**:154:**168**:180), p2tog, p1. *384(**412**:444:**484**:516) sts*

These 4 rounds set yoke dec and garter st in the round.

Cont working garter st in the round as set above WHILST AT THE SAME TIME working yoke dec every third row (as set above) a further 26(**25**:27:**30**:33) times more. *176(**212**:228:**244**:252) sts*

Second size only

Work 3 rounds straight in garter st.

All sizes

Keep garter st in the round as set throughout, work as folls:

Next round: Work garter st in the round as set over next 8(**10**:10:**10**:8) sts, SM, [k1, sk2po] 20(**24**:26:**28**:29) times, k0(**0**:0:**0**:2), SM, work garter st in the round as set over next 8(**10**:10:**10**:8) sts, SM, [k1, sk2po] 20(**24**:26:**28**:29) times, k0(**0**:0:**0**:2). *96(**112**:124:**132**:140) sts*

Fourth and fifth sizes only

Work garter st in the round as set over next –(–:–:**10**:8) sts, SM, [k–:–:–:**6**:4, k2tog, k–:–:–:**6**:4] –(–:–:**4**:6) times, SM, work garter st in the round as set over next –(–:–:**10**:8) sts, SM, [k–:–:–:**6**:4, k2tog, k–:–:–:**6**:4] –(–:–:**4**:15) times. *–(–:–:**124**:124) sts*

All sizes

*96(**112**:124:**124**:124) sts*

Now work in rib as foll:

Rib round: *K2, p2; rep from * to end.

Cont until rib measures approx. 5cm (2in).

Cast (bind) off in rib.

FINISHING

Press/block all garment pieces.

Join both side seams approx. 14cm (5½in) down from each underarm, then join underarm and sleeve seams using mattress stitch or preferred method.

Now work the darning on each part of garment, being creative and using the photographs as a guide (see also Hints and Tips). Cut lengths of B, 8cm (3in) longer than the part of the garment you are working on, and work under and over the garter stitch ridges throughout, creating three stripes together. Continue over entire garment to create a faux tartan design.

Fasten off any loose ends.

Press/block again if needed.

HINTS AND TIPS
▶ **Darning method**
Once you have completed the garment you will have the horizontal stripes of your tartan pattern; now it's time to add the vertical stripes. Work from the cast-off (bound-off) edge to the shoulder, neck or sleeve head of the garment.

⦿ You have the opportunity to become really creative here and design your own tartan placement. As suggested in the pattern you can use the photographs as a guide but there is no right or wrong place to work the darning... so go wild!

❯ Spread out, and work on a large surface – this way you can clearly work out where you want to place your vertical stripes. You could use pins to plan out each vertical stripe.

DAISY

[RAGLAN | Fairisle Yoke Sweater]

A fairisle yoke always sits nicer with a little bit of short row shaping. This is placed before the charts even come into play, making it a much easier way of getting that beautiful yoke silhouette.

TECHNIQUE
Fairisle in the round with decreases and short row shaping

SIZE Note sizes are approximate.

	Small	Medium	Large	X Large	XX Large	
To fit	81–86	91–96	101–106	112–117	122–127	cm
	32–34	36–38	40–42	44–46	48–50	in
Actual	113	122	131	140	153	cm
(approx.)	44½	48	51½	55	60	in
Length	56	56	58	58	60	cm
(approx.)	22	22	23	23	23½	in
Sleeve seam	43	45.5	47	47	49	cm
(approx.)	17	18	18½	18½	19¼	in

YARN
Aran (worsted)
Sample made in
Erika Knight Vintage Wool
(100% British Wool, approx. 87m/96yd
per 50g/1¾oz ball)
9(**9**:10:**11**:12) balls of Dark (**A**)
1(**1**:1:**2**:2) balls of Mulberry (**B**)
1(**1**:1:**2**:2) balls of Flax (**C**)
1(**1**:1:**2**:2) balls of Leighton (**D**)
1(**1**:1:**2**:2) balls of Wisteria (**E**)

NEEDLES AND OTHER ITEMS
5mm (US size 8) straight needles
5mm (US size 8) long circular needle
3 large stitch holders
4 stitch markers

TENSION (GAUGE)
18 sts x 24 rows = 10cm (4in) square
working st st on 5mm (US size 8) needles.

ABBREVIATIONS
See page 20

PATTERN NOTE
When working charts A, B, C and D for the yoke in rounds, read each row of the chart from right to left. When working chart E on straight needles, read all odd number (RS) rows from right to left and even number (WS) rows from left to right.

CHART A

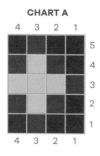

CHART B

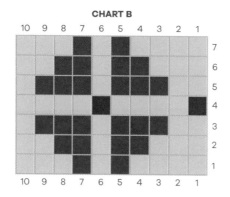

CHART C

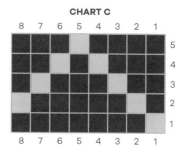

CHART D

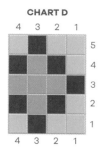

CHART E

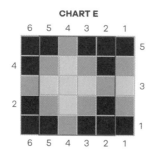

KEY

☐	Rnds/Rows
■	A: Dark
■	B: Mulberry
■	C: Flax
■	D: Leighton
■	E: Wisteria
☐	Patt Repeat

MAKE

BACK/FRONT
(make both the same to armholes)
Using 5mm (US size 8) straight needles and
A, cast on 102(**110**:118:**126**:138) sts.
Row 1 (RS): *K1, p1; rep from * to end.
Row 2: As Row 1.
These 2 rows rep form rib.
Cont in rib until work measures approx. 5cm
(2in) from cast-on edge, ending with RS facing.
Now work in st st as folls:
Row 1: K.
Row 2: P.
These 2 rows rep form st st.
Cont in st st until work measures approx.
32:**32**:34:**34**:36cm (12½:**12½**:13½:**13½**:14in),
ending with RS facing.
Working in st st, cast (bind) off 8 sts at beg
of next 2 rows. *86(**94**:102:**110**:122) sts*
Leave rem sts on a holder.

SLEEVES (make 2)
Using 5mm (US size 8) straight needles and
B, cast on 34(**34**:38:**38**:42) sts.
Row 1 (RS): *K1, p1; rep from * to end.
Row 2: As Row 1.
These 2 rows rep form rib.
Cont in rib until work measures approx. 5cm
(2in) from cast-on edge, ending with RS facing.
Now place Chart E and introduce yarns A, D
and E as folls:
(take care not to pull yarn too tightly when
working fairisle method)
Chart row 1: K1 A, *k2 A, k1 D, k1 A; rep from
* to last st, k1 A.
Chart row 2: P1 A, *p1 D, p1 E, p1 D, p1 A; rep
from * to last st, p1 D.
Cont working from Chart E as set above,

working all 5 chart rows, ending with **WS** facing.
Cont in A only.
Next row (WS): P.
Now work in st st as folls:
Row 1: K.
Row 2: P.
These 2 rows rep form st st.
Cont in st st WHILST AT THE SAME TIME inc
1 st at each end of next and then every sixth
rowto 58(**58**:62:**64**:68) sts, ending with RS facing.
Cont straight in st st until work measures
43:**45.5**:47:**47**:49cm (17:**18**:18½:**18½**:19¼in), ending
with RS facing.
Working in st st, cast (bind) off 8 sts at beg of
next 2 rows. *42(**42**:46:**48**:52) sts*
Leave rem sts on a holder.

YOKE
Now join all garment pieces to form yoke, working
in rounds. PM to indicate beg/end of round (slip at
beg of each round).
Using 5mm (US size 8) circular needle, re-join yarn
and k across 42(**42**:46:**48**:52) sts for first sleeve
using A, PM, k across 86(**94**:102:**110**:122) sts for front,
PM, k across 42(**42**:46:**48**:52) sts for second sleeve
using A, PM, and then k across 86(**94**:102:**110**:122)
sts for back using A. *256(**272**:296:**316**:348) sts*
Beg short row shaping
K to first marker, SM, k14, wrap next st, turn, p to
beg/end marker, p142(**150**:162:**172**:188) slipping
markers, wrap next st, turn, k193(**201**:217:**229**:249)
slipping markers, wrap next st, turn,
p188(**196**:212:**224**:244) slipping markers, wrap next
st, turn, k183(**191**:207:**219**:239) slipping markers,
wrap next st, turn, p178(**186**:202:**214**:234) slipping
markers, wrap next st, turn, k132(**140**:152:**162**:178).

You will now be back at beg/end marker, cont in rounds.

Now work yoke dec as folls:

Yoke round 1: K1, ssk, k to 3 sts before next marker, k2tog, k1, SM, k1, ssk, k to 3 sts before next marker, k2tog, k1, SM, k1, ssk, k to 3 sts before next marker, k2tog, k1, SM, k1, ssk, k to 3 sts before next marker, k2tog, k1. *248(**264**:288:**308**:340) sts*

Yoke round 2: K to first marker, SM, k to second marker, SM marker, k to third marker, SM, k to end. Rep these 2 yoke rounds 7(**9**:11:**13**:15) times more. *192(**192**:200:**204**:220) sts*

Now work Chart A as folls:

Chart round 1: *K2 A, k1 B, k1 A; rep from * to end.

Chart round 2: *K1 A, k1 B, k1 C, k1 B; rep from * to end.

Cont working from Chart A as set above, working all 5 chart rounds.

Change to A.

K 1 round.

Change to D.

K 1 round.

Now work Yoke Round 1 as set above. *184(**184**:192:**196**:212) sts*

Change to E.

First and second sizes only

Next round (dec): K to first marker, SM, k1, ssk, k to 3 sts before next marker, k2tog, k1, SM, knit to third marker, SM, k1, ssk, k to 3 sts before next marker, k2tog, k1. *180(**180**:–:–:–) sts*

Third and fifth sizes only

Next rond (dec): K to first marker, SM, k1, ssk, k to 3 sts before next marker, k2tog, k1, SM, knit to third marker, SM, k1, k to 3 sts before next marker, k1. *–(–:**190**:–:210) sts*

Fourth size only

Next round (dec): K to first marker, SM, k1, [ssk] twice, k to 5 sts before next marker, [k2tog] twice, k1, SM, knit to third marker, SM, k1, ssk, k to 3 sts before next marker, k2tog, k1. *–(–:–:**190**:–) sts*

All sizes

*180(**180**:190:**190**:210) sts*

Now work Chart B as folls:

Chart round 1: *K4 E, k1 B, k1 E, k1 B, k3 E; rep from * to end.

Chart round 2: *K3 E, k2 B, k1 E, k2 B, k2 E; rep from * to end.

Cont working from Chart B as set above, working all 7 chart rounds.

Change to E.

K 1 round.

Change to D.

K 1 round.

First and second sizes only

Next round (dec): *K6, sk2po; rep from * to end. *140(**140**:–:–:–) sts*

Third and fourth sizes only

Next round (dec): *K6, sk2po; rep from * to last st, k1. *–(–:148:**148**:–) sts*

Fifth size only

Next round (dec): K10, [sk2po, k4] 14 times, k11, [sk2po, k4] 13 times. *–(–:–:–:156) sts*

All sizes

*140(**140**:148:**148**:156) sts*

Next round (dec): K to first marker, SM, k1, ssk, k to 3 sts before next marker, k2tog, k1, SM, knit to third marker, SM, k1, ssk, k to 3 sts before next marker, k2tog, k1. *136(**136**:144:**144**:152) sts*

Now work Chart C as folls:

Chart round 1: *K1 E, k7 A; rep from * to end.

Chart round 2: *K1 A, k1 E, k5 A, k1 E; rep from * to end.

Cont working from Chart C as set above, working all 5 chart rounds.

Change to C.

K 1 round.

Now work Yoke Round 1 as set above.

*128(**128**:136:**136**:144) sts*

Now work Chart D as folls:

Chart round 1: *K2 C, k1 B, k1 C; rep from * to end.

Chart round 2: *K1 C, k1 B, k1 C, k1 B; rep from * to end.

Cont working from Chart D as set above, working all 5 chart rounds.

Change to D.

K 1 round.

Work Yoke Round 1 as set above.

*120(**120**:128:**128**:136) sts*

Next round (dec): *K5, sk2po; rep from * to end.

*90(**90**:96:**96**:102) sts*

Change to A.

Knitter's note: If neck is wider than you would prefer, replace the next knit round with a further decrease round: you could work another Yoke Round 1 and decrease a further 8 sts.

Next round: K.

Now work in rib as folls:

Rib round: *K1, p1; rep from * to end.

Cont until rib measures approx. 3cm (1¼in).

Cast (bind) off in rib.

FINISHING

Press/block all garment pieces.

Join side, underarm and sleeve seams using mattress stitch or preferred method.

Fasten off any loose ends.

Press/block again if needed.

HINTS AND TIPS

▶ When decreasing in the round it's important to work the k2tog and ssk where stated within a pattern because these decreases will slant in the correct direction to form the yoke.

⊙ When working the fairisle you need to keep a tight and even tension – but if you pull too tightly your work will pucker and look uneven. Remember to strand your yarn at the back leaving enough length so that the fabric in front can sit flat and even.

◗ Always wrap your last stitch when turning your work during short row shaping to prevent a hole.

BLANK MODELS

Experiment by creating your own colourways and sweater designs using the principles in this book.

I can't wait to see what you make from this book. Please use the hashtag #emmaknitted to share snaps of your creations on Instagram.

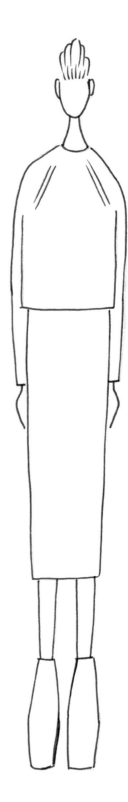

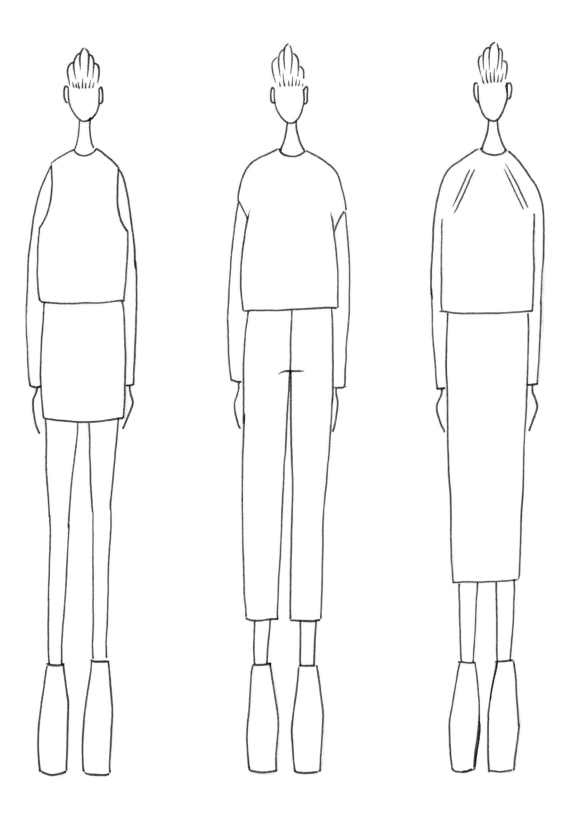

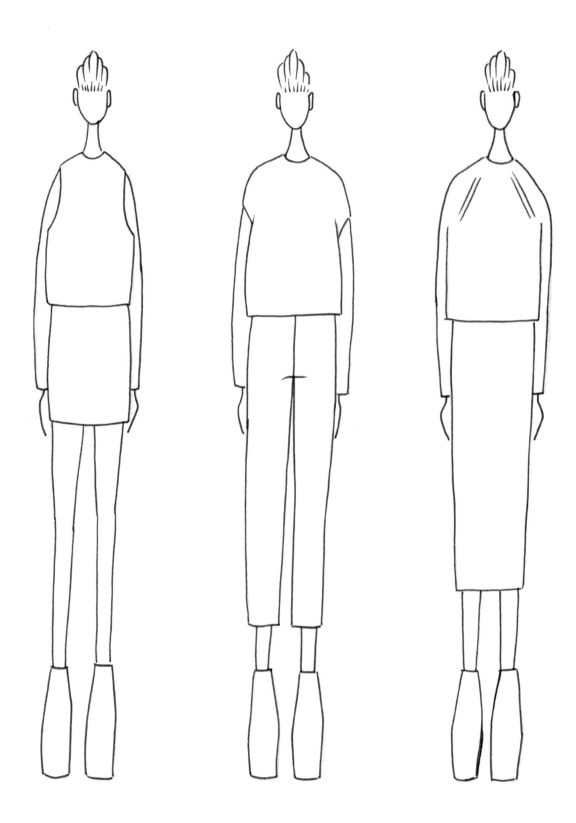

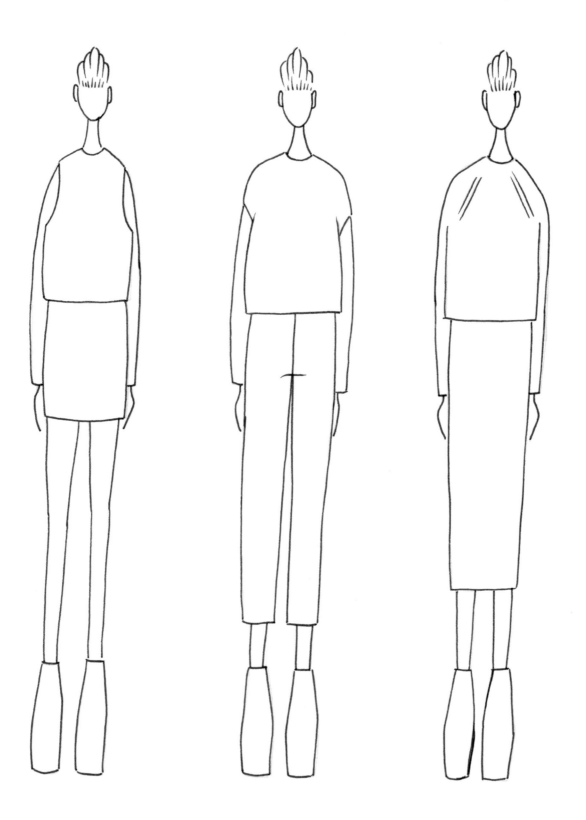

ACKNOWLEDGEMENTS

As a teenager my dream was to write my own knitting book: sixteen-year-old me, we did it!

I am forever appreciative to Quadrille Publishing for seeing my potential; it has been an honour to work with you all. I would especially like to thank my Commissioning editor, Harriet Butt, for your time, effort and patience. Also for allowing me to bring my new baby and his daddy along with me to London while we did the shoot – a son and daddy time they will never forget. We finished this book through having my first baby, as well as lockdown, with yet more patience, understanding and encouragement from Harriet – I am forever grateful! A huge thank you to Katherine Keeble who I am sure has been inside my head and laid this book out exactly as I had envisaged, from the colour palette to the small details.

To my wonderful knitters, both my Nans (June and Mabel), Cheryl, Gwen and Sarah – your knitting is beautiful and always perfect. I owe everything to my Nan June, who knits for me at the speed of light under the most ridiculous deadlines and never bats an eyelid.

I would also like to thank Kim Lightbody for photographs of my work that I could only dream of. Thank you to the brilliant models Chelsea, Tatiana and Erika – you brought my designs to life – to Jenni for glowing hair and make-up, and to Marie for perfectly editing and proofreading my patterns.

Thank you to Erika Knight for your continued support as well as your generous yarn contributions for my designs. I would also like to thank Lovecraft, Rowan Yarns, Debbie Bliss, The Fibre Co. and West Yorkshire Spinners for their generosity in supplying yarns for the projects within this book.

I am indebted to my wonderful family, who have gone above and beyond for me over the years. My mum, who drove me to the station every day for four years when I commuted to university; my dad, who often paid for the train fare; my granddad, who has fixed my knitting machines and made me many design contraptions over the years; my sister Issy, who always proofreads my work – and of course every other member of my family, there is not enough room in this book to write the amount of wonderful things you have done for me. Finally, to the other half of me, Lewis: without you none of this is possible. You encourage and inspire me. I think we have the wonders of Fortnite to thank for your patience when I've spent all day, night and weekends working.

Emma x

ABOUT THE AUTHOR

Emma Wright is a fashion, knit and crochet designer. She is heavily influenced by colour and floral patterns, which is reflected through the playfulness of her designs.

Sine graduating in 2014, she turned emmaknitted into a full-time business, designing knit and crochet patterns for yarn brands and magazines in the industry. Emma was subsequently awarded the coverted 'Britain Next Top Knitwear Designer' by Lovecrafts. Emma lives just outside of Sheffield with her partner, Lewis, and son Max.

@emmaknitted

Publishing Director Sarah Lavelle
Senior Commissioning Editor Harriet Butt
Design and Art Direction Katherine Keeble
Stylist Charlotte Melling
Prop stylist Faye Wears
Photographer Kim Lightbody
Head of Production Stephen Lang
Senior Production Controller Katie Jarvis

Published in 2020 by Quadrille,
an imprint of Hardie Grant Publishing

Quadrille
52–54 Southwark Street
London SE1 1UN
quadrille.com

Cataloguing in Publication Data: a catalogue record for this book is available from the British Library.

text © Emma Wright 2020
photography © Kim Lightbody 2020
design © Quadrille 2020

ISBN 978 1 78713 476 8

Printed in China

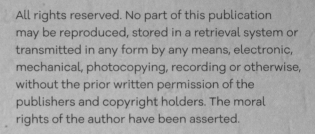